JACKSON HOLE JOURNAL

The Tetons from the Bar BC. Courtesy of George Vaux, ARPS, Bryn Mawr, Pa.

JACKSON HOLE JOURNAL

By Nathaniel Burt

NORMAN : UNIVERSITY OF OKLAHOMA PRESS

By Nathaniel Burt

Rooms in a House (New York, 1947)
Question on a Kite (New York, 1950)
Scotland's Burning (Boston, 1953)
Make My Bed (Boston, 1957)
The Perennial Philadelphians (Boston, 1963)
War Cry of the West (New York, 1964)
Leopards in the Garden (Boston, 1968)
First Families (Boston, 1970)
Palaces for the People (Boston, 1977)

Library of Congress Cataloging in Publication Data

Burt, Nathaniel, 1913–
  Jackson Hole journal.

  Includes index.
  1. Burt, Nathaniel, 1913–   . 2. Jackson Hole (Wyo.) — Social life
and customs. 3. Dude ranches — Wyoming — Jackson Hole. 4. Jackson
Hole (Wyo.) — Biography. I. Title.
F767.T28B873   1983   978.7'55   83-47831

To my sister
Julia Burt Atteberry

CONTENTS

ILLUSTRATIONS

MAP

PART ONE: In the Beginning, 1910–1930

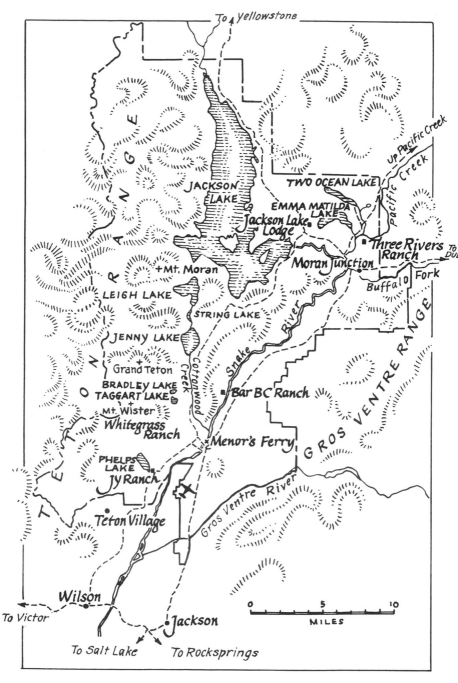

Jackson Hole, Wyoming

1.

PRELUDES

THIS is in no sense another "history of Jackson Hole"; it is, rather, an autobiography with digressions. Having kept a journal of summers spent in Jackson Hole—beginning in 1928 and extending to the present—I thought that the diary itself might serve as a chronicle of the place and times. On looking it over, however, I saw that it did not—too personal and, without extensive explanations, too cryptic. This book, then, is another kind of journal on the order of my father's *Diary of a Dude Wrangler*, one that supplies the explanations without giving more than a few excerpts of the original diary. It does not pretend to be a picture of everybody's Jackson Hole, just mine. It does not pretend to be accurate history, just my memories and the legends I was told.

Jackson Hole is a valley in the northwest corner of Wyoming, just below Yellowstone National Park. On the west Jackson Hole is bounded by the high, bare, jagged range of the Tetons, now included in Grand Teton National Park. Most of the flat, bare, sagebrush-covered floor of the valley (Jackson Hole itself) is also in the park. To the east Jackson Hole is bounded by a gentler range of mountains, properly spelled Gros Ventres ("big bellies" in trapper French, as the Tetons are "tits") but always pronounced Grovont, which is how I write it. Lesser mountains also close off the north and south, thus forming what trappers referred to as a "hole" or "basin." The only town of any size is Jackson. Thus the valley is Jackson Hole, but the town is just Jackson. They are both named after a nondescript trapper of the early nineteenth century.

When I was little, nobody had ever heard of Jackson Hole. Nowadays hardly a year passes without the Tetons being used for some national advertising campaign. The Grand Teton must be one of the most-photographed mountains in the United States, and the Tetons themselves have joined Niagara Falls and the Grand Canyon as one of the "sights" of America.

Jackson Hole was once approachable only by railroad from Victor, Idaho, and then by a rough, steep road over the mountains (always called simply "the Pass"). Five good, big highways now bring in 3 million visitors every summer. In winter there are thousands of skiers—when the snow is propitious. Remoteness, one of the chief charms of the early Hole, is no longer characteristic. Thanks to the park and the Wilderness Areas of the United States Forest Service, a lot of it is still wild. But for the Jackson Hole native it is difficult to reconcile the secluded frontier of the 1920s to the tourist-boom center of today. It is like having your childhood sweetheart become a movie star on the grand old-fashioned scale of a Greta Garbo.

Wyoming still remains one of the least-populated states in the Union. Of its roughly half a million present inhabitants, only a small fraction were born there. Of the some seven thousand citizens of Jackson Hole itself, even a smaller fraction are native-born. Of this fraction I am one.

I became a native on November 21, 1913, on my father's ranch, the Bar B C. Located almost in the geographical center of the valley, the Bar B C was the second of the Hole's dude ranches. It was built on the banks of the Snake River, due east of the Grand Teton, and a few miles above what is now

Moose, headquarters of the park, then called Menor's Ferry (pronounced "Meenor"). To us on the ranch it seemed the hub of the universe, the center of a kingdom that was mostly wilderness stretching in every direction, and which we felt was ours, all ours, as far as the eye or the fancy could reach.

I passed my first and my third winters on the Bar B C. My earliest ranch memory is of the second of those winters. The snow was five feet deep. I was standing outside the cabin in the morning sun — the whole long, low, L-shaped cabin buried to the eaves. Tunnels had been dug down to the doors, but I could not seem to find them. I was lost, marooned, alone, unable to imagine my way back in.

This small vignette of isolation is the one impression of my first winters of which I can be sure, the one memory that I know is my own, not something told me by someone else. I don't remember, for instance, running over the snow crust, thick enough to hold me but not an adult, towards the river and meeting face-to-face with a huge bull moose. I don't re-member Christmas trees lit by real candles in the dark, low cabin, though I remember vividly the cheap, metal clip-on candleholders in tinsel, pastel colors. I don't remember any people at all. The ranch cook made twisted sticks of yellow molasses candy for me. I remember vividly the shape of them and the molasses taste, but I don't remember the cook.

Joe LePage, the foreman at the Bar B C, was surely there, and I remember him, if only perhaps from a later time. There were, I know, winter dudes. Francis Biddle (later attorney gen-eral of the United States under Franklin D. Roosevelt) was one of them, paying court to my Aunt Jean Burt, though already involved with his future wife. He describes it all in his autobiographical *Casual Past*. My father's partner, Dr. Horace Carncross, pupil of Anna Freud in psychiatry, was surely there. My sister Julia was born at the beginning of my second winter in the Hole, on September 30, 1915. I became two in November. And I remember—I *think* I remember— bedtime in a little room of my own, off the big room where my parents and Julie slept in what was later on the main-cabin living room of the Bar B C. Candlelight, me rocking back and forth and singing one of two favorites: "*Je*-sus *ten*-der *leo*-pard *hear* me," or "Good-bye girls I'm *through*, I've had enough of *you*." Beyond the open door a big wicker clothes basket stood next to my mother's bed on the other side of the living room fireplace. This was Julie's crib. It was decorated with ribbons. But could this really have been so early, that winter of 1915, my second on the ranch? It might have been a year later perhaps, in late fall, certainly not summer, when we Burts lived in our own, separate cabin.

It was of course not 1913, the year of my birth. My father and mother had been married that spring in Princeton, New Jersey. My father brought my mother as a bride to his new homestead down by the Snake River. For several years he had been the partner of Lew Joy on his dude ranch, the JY on Phelps Lake, the first in the Hole; but they had not got on. Joy was a secretive, difficult man. Nobody much seems to remember him now, and my father seldom spoke of him, and then not kindly. He certainly wrote of him bitterly in his *Diary of a Dude Wrangler*. Still, Joy was the first dude rancher in the valley, and a successful one. It was to the JY that Owen Wister came, while his own cabin on his own ranch, also down along the Snake, was being built; and it was at the JY that my father knew Wister, rode with him, listened to his some-times melancholy soliloquies. "I have never known a moment's happiness," he said of himself to my father, unbelievably— the then so famous author, the social lion, the close friend of Theodore Roosevelt and Henry Adams and Henry James.

The homesteading of the Bar B C was a breakaway for my father, a rash venture based on almost no capital and many fond dreams. Though intended from the first as a dude ranch — that bastard of East and West — the real hope, eventually realized, was to have it part of a cattle ranch, the real thing, the sign and symbol of true Western aristocracy.

I wouldn't want to try for accuracy about just which dudes came first and just when. The first six arrived the year before I was born, in the summer of 1912, coming in with my mother on her first trip west as my father's fiancée. It was a group of older young people (my father was already over thirty in 1912), most of them with Princeton and Philadelphia connections, talented, sophisticated, very much liberated prewar post-Edwardians, full of advanced tinges of Freud and the Impressionists and fin de siècle English literature, but Romantics to a man and woman. It was because the West was so Romantic that they were there — the West, incredibly beautiful of course, then as now, with all the natural panoply of sun and sky and air, of mountains and flowers and streams and game — but above all, in those days and from the point of view of nowadays, incredibly, inconceivably remote.

This group, this small clique of semipermanent picnickers, couldn't have been further from base if the locale had been Tibet.

Francis Biddle's psychiatrist brother, Sydney, like Carncross a disciple of Freud; Tucker Bispham, most-elegant disciple of Max Beerbohm; and Adolph Borie, painter and far-off disciple of Renoir, were among the first of this group. Others were three Chicagoans: the painter Abram Poole, a college roommate of my father; the fashionable architect David Adler; and their mutual friend George Porter. Tucker wrote Swinburnian poetry, and in prewar Oxford was followed at ten paces by his valet Nurser. After a hard night Tucker would recline languidly on a sofa and murmur, "Bring me something, Nurser." Adolph Borie became official portraitist to Philadelphia, doing sober likenesses of worthies when he would rather have been doing Impressionist oils. He helped build the cobblestone chimneys of the very low sod-roofed log cabins and played the guitar. Adler and Poole were in the social circles of the young Adlai Stevenson and through them my parents got to know the statesman and his wife.

My father's sister Jean—who also, like Borie, played the guitar—sang songs of her own composition, words and music, rather dreadfully evocative of cowboy ballads, full of horses. She idolized horses and rode with passion and skill, out West and in Virginia. She was a small, dark, vivacious, nervous, sentimental woman, full of charm but fractious and very jealous of my mother. Her rival for the affections of the male bunch was another aunt of mine, my mother's sister Mary Newlin. Polly (Aunt Paul, I always called her) was red-haired, willowy, throaty-voiced, a sort of half-unwilling and half-unconscious femme fatale who stole Tucker and Sydney and others away from Jean so that there were rival camps, amorous tensions, feuds and dramas. Tucker's poem to Polly, beginning, "Red ruinous roses / growing under the sea," sets the prewar period and mood of it all.

These intrigues and passions flourished especially in winter, when those that were still on the ranch were cooped up together for days at a time by blizzards. In one of those I was born, my mother on a kitchen table attended by Dr. Carncross, student of Freud, while my father was out somewhere rounding up horses in the snow. Born in a log-cabin kitchen, delivered by a psychiatrist—it was a picturesque enough blend of dude and roughneck, West and East, Leatherstocking and Silkstocking. I assume there were kettles of water boiling on the wood-burning kitchen ranges for whatever purposes such kettles boil.

For years, for twenty years perhaps, it was this blend of wildness and sophistication, of remoteness and civilization that gave Jackson Hole and especially the Bar B C a special quality. It was not just that the Hole was wild and full of cowboys and people who shot their friends and enemies (though rather rarely, in fact) and old-timers and former outlaws and hermit recluses and wicked local bankers; but also that it had Owen Wister and Cadwaladers and Biddles and Peabodys of Groton and a whole string of fierce ladies of high degree. Eleanor Patterson, always called "the Countess," was the first and most conspicuous of those who began as dudes but became ranchers and raised cattle and hell (some of them), had affairs (some of them) with their foremen, and always had style.

It was a classless society full of class, where the swagger of Western horsemen blended on equal terms with the swagger of adventurous, anticonventional Eastern aristocracy. Everyone—ranchers, Jackson storekeepers, hired hands, dudes— was caught up in this society, involved in the intense feuds and friendships, the bitter causes (park extension and related problems), took sides, cheated each other selling horses and playing poker, loved, hated, even married each other. Every other ranch, particularly down the west side of the Snake River, was owned by an old dude of the JY or the Bar B C or the later White Grass. Owen Wister, Lambert Cadwalader, and the Countess up Flat Creek were merely among the earliest.

Miss Noble, who looked like a handsome, female George Washington with her white, cropped hair and riding britches, and her former English coachman Sidney Sandal ran the store down at Menor's Ferry, now Moose. The town of Wilson was some twenty miles downstream, and Sheffield's place at the dam (Moran) some twenty miles upstream. The ferry was the only way across the river in midvalley, a real ferry then. Nobody knew whether Miss Noble and Sidney slept together or not, but they had certainly run away from Philadelphia together. She was always "Miss Noble" to him; he was always "Sidney" to her.

About every five years some dude girl would marry a cowboy and settle down in the valley, nobody more successfully than Frances and Buster Estes. People would come out from the East to work on a ranch, like Frank and Gertie Bessette on the Bar B C, and become first citizens; or Westerners would be working on the ranch, meet and marry and end up hotel-owning millionaires like the Worts. Unlike a middle-class society where everyone has to kowtow to a norm to avoid the offenses of superiority — a Middle Western democracy based on the equality of everyone being alike — people in the old Jackson Hole remained separate but equal, flamboyantly themselves without fear of what the neighbors might think; it was the classlessness of individuality — a Far Western democracy based on everyone being different.

It was the remoteness that did it. There was nobody around to mediate between dudes and roughnecks, countesses and cowboys, shut up together in their cantankerous Shangri-la. All through my childhood you had to allow at least a day just to get in or out of the Hole. The only real connection with the world then was across Teton Pass to that little fag-end railroad town of Victor, in Idaho. Even when automobiles first came in, about the beginning of the twenties, it was a good long half-day trip from the ranch to Victor over the narrow, steep, room-for-one-car dirt road. I remember the ranch truck turning a corner too widely so that a rear wheel went over the edge. We all got out, ruminated, pushed the car back on the road. Once on the train, you spent the later afternoon moseying up to Ashton with stops at Driggs and Tetonia, then the night back down through Idaho to Salt Lake and transcontinental trains.

When my mother first came out as a fiancée the year before I was born, she got off the train at Saint Anthony, north of Victor (where the line then stopped), and got into a wagon. That trip usually took three days—a night in Victor at the Killpack Hotel, another night at Wilson, and finally the ranch. My own first and vivid memories were of these wagon trips; but by my time the railroad had been built down to its final destination in Victor. There were always vague threats of putting the railroad right through into Jackson Hole itself.

Victor was considered a sort of boomtown, the vanguard of Progress. When my father had first come to the Hole before 1910, the country to the west of the Tetons was all tawny sheep range. Between then and 1920 it was taken up by farmers, many of them Mormon (Vardis Fisher, bardic novelist of Mormonism, was born in Saint Anthony) who developed a whole string of small towns—Victor, Driggs, Drummond, Tetonia—along the brand-new spur of railroad. By now, this area has become a green, somnolent backwater. The towns lie stranded, the railroad carries freight only (if it runs at all), the tourist traffic goes around through to Yellowstone or Jackson Hole. Victor and its sister cities that once represented encroaching Civilization are now residually quaint Old West, waiting to be exploited as such. (It was the northern part of this area that was devastated by the Teton Dam break and flood in the spring of 1976.)

When we came out, late in May or early in June, there was usually snow on the pass, so the wheels were taken off the wagon and runners put on to make a sleigh to go over the top. The particular trip I remember got into trouble. The wagon-sleigh started to slip slowly over the curve of the snowy edge. We all hopped out, and I have the fantastic but very clear image of my Burt grandmother and myself both clinging to the edge of the wagon, trying to prevent it from disaster. Evidently we failed, because we had to walk through slush to the top of the pass and I got blisters on my heels from tramping in my galoshes.

In those first days we always spent the night in Wilson where a peaked-roof log hotel was originally kept by a charming former badman called, I believe, McCoy. As usual I remember nothing of the people. Instead I was enthralled by a big wooden waterwheel and by big white fierce geese, the only ones I ever saw or heard of in the Hole. Then the long hot trip up the west side of the valley, first through the settled green hay-fields of Mosquito Flats, then through the woods and over the rickety board bridges across rushing cold outlets from lakes, then back onto the flats again and finally east, on our own cobble-rough road, towards the Bar B C in its river valley.

You couldn't see the ranch as you started toward the Gro-vonts, with the Tetons and evening at your back. It looked as though you would have to travel straight across the valley for hot miles of sagebrush to those further mountains. Then suddenly came the second bench, a prehistoric riverbank, run-ning neat as a dam north and south, then the steep road down a gully in the jolting wagon between larkspur and mule-ears, with perhaps a last decadent little snowbank still lingering in the draw—the whole panorama of river valley opening out below. Then finally you came down the first bench right into the ranch itself—the sod or tar-paper-roofed cabins, the corrals and saddle shed and barns and ditches and willows and big pines and aspen groves and the shining square of the swimming pool dug out of the flat between cabins and river. It was suppertime by then, no dudes yet, but the outfit would be on hand—Joe LePage, the foreman, and whatever cook could be managed, and a wrangler or two at least.

It was coming home with a vengeance, Traveler's Rest with a vengeance. What a trip it must have been for my mother, either pregnant and by wagon from Idaho, or later on with two wildly active and eternally inventive children. It took about six days on a train through the summer Middle West with no air conditioning and windows that opened to the blasts of baked prairie heat and cinders from the steam engines.

The trip would usually begin in Philadelphia, from the dark sooty cavern of the old Broad Street Station, overnight to Chicago. There we usually spent the next night with Mrs. Waller and her daughter in Oak Forest—a castle of miracles where I rolled great balls up and down the private bowling alley and Mrs. Waller would produce for us from a closet, Aladdin's own cave, oriental presents, big Japanese parasols or tiny good-luck toy chow dogs (I still have them). Then back on board for the two-night trip to Salt Lake.

Another break came at the Utah Hotel, lap of luxury, which seemed to be constructed outside and in of white bathroom tiling—white outside in the curious turn of the century semi-classic skyscraperese (common in Western cities), white inside with a black-and-white-tiled lobby, edged with what I remember as a design of swastikas. (What did they do about that after

1941? Or did anybody notice? Or were they really swastikas?) There were great white bathrooms and bathtubs, last of the summer for us going West, first of the fall for us going East. The Utah hotel was my initial experience of an elevator, which I called a "little cabin that goes up." Then finally, next afternoon, we boarded the overnight train up to Victor, arriving in the morning for the total excitement of the Teton range emerging, turned backwards, over the Idaho foothills; and then at last came the disembarkation to the waiting wagon, or, later on, the truck.

The trip was miserable, enthralling, exhausting, an experience – the observation platform at the end of the train with its little green-serge folding stools where cinders got into your eye (to be removed by a loop of human hair) and strange gentlemen smoking cigars jovially teased you; the elaborate meals in the dining car, always endlessly far away through many heavy Pullman doors, the joggling lurching table covered with rich linen and silver plate, the squares of ice cream in three colors accompanied by brittle, sweet Nabisco wafers; the whooshing by of towns with a melancholy downward wail of their railroad crossing bells, the endless flick of telegraph poles. Each day we were given a present, usually a game of some sort (jackstraws, a ticklish sport for a swaying Pullman car). Eventually the hot day would reach a climax of lost tempers, thumbs mashed in washroom doors, specks in the eye, total coverage of soot; but I loved every single minute of it.

And then, finally, like the end of an ocean voyage, the blessed clean, cool quietness of the ranch, loud at night with the sound of the river, brilliant by day with flowers and butterflies.

No wonder that when Easterners went through all that they felt that they had gotten somewhere, somewhere important, exotic, isolated and special, well worth the trip, but on the other hand made worthwhile by that trip. A whole world existed up to the 1930s almost without automobiles, electricity, telephones, or plumbing, connected to the nearest town, Jackson, by an endless dusty road and the river-current-operated, board-floored wooden ferry, a world connected in turn to the outside only by erratic Western Union from Jackson, or the rackety railroad from Victor.

So that when people got there, they stayed there. The town of Jackson itself was an arduous trip from the Bar B C. I remember that trip by wagon—with a ford, not a bridge, across the Grovont River near Kelly. Jackson was the only real settlement—from 1923 on, the seat of the new Teton County—carved out of enormous Lincoln County with its seat way south in Kemmerer, which in turn had been part of even greater Uinta, the whole southwestern corner of the state.

On the map, however, there were always Wilson, then as now a few roadside cabins like McCoy's hotel, the second city or Chicago of the Hole; Kelly, a log-cabin store and church and school on the Grovont River; Menor's Ferry with the Noble store and cabin and the ferry run by Bill Menor; Elk, a movable post office that served the group of ranchers up the Buffalo Fork; Moran, the settlement at the foot of Jackson Lake dam, near which had once been a mysterious "Conrad's Ferry" always on older maps; and finally the even more mysterious Zenith on the east side at the junction of the Grovont and Snake, which must have once been a post office, but which I never heard of in real life.

We did go to Jackson, even in earlier days, despite the long trip, especially at rodeo time in late August or early September. Usually, we were stuck within riding distance of the ranch, Menor's Ferry (for small purchases and the post office), and the neighboring ranches (especially those other two dude ranches, the JY and the White Grass). We relied on these for outside company.

The Bar B C was its own isolated community; friendships and feuds developed there quickly under the pressures of that isolation. Love affairs smouldered and blazed — there is a whole series of Bar B C marriages — everyone's character emerged under a magnifying glass; the true colors came out like stones under water. The arrivals of new dudes, the departures of old ones were tremendous events. Hands quit, usually with many a harsh word and sinister imputation, cabin girls and dude girls vied for the attention of wranglers — usually good looking in exact inverse ratio to their usefulness. Oriental cooks eventually became permanently established and staged sudden nightlong binges based on homemade raisin wine that led to chases around the kitchen with knives. Never a dull moment.

Nobody then, before the thirties, had ever heard of Jackson Hole in the world outside, except for a few big-game hunters, and of course our dudes. People thought the word "Hole" screamingly funny, and you had to give an illustration of where it was in relation to Yellowstone Park, the Hole's northern neighbor — the park as a postage stamp in the wrong corner of the envelope of Wyoming, Jackson Hole vaguely down below. People had heard of Yellowstone, all right, but even maps would get the Hole all wrong and have the Snake River running down in some impossible way. People would say, "Is it in the mountains?" and would look blank when you mentioned the Tetons.

There were, true enough, two dangerous, narrow, rain-slippery, washed-away-by-slides other roads out eastward over the Hoback and Togwotee (pronounced "TOE-ge-tee") Pass;

but they led only to Pinedale and Dubois (pronounced DUbois, not DuBOIS, or God help us, French "dubwah"). One of the funniest things about dudes was their mispronunciation of words like Mon-*tah*-na, though I noticed we all said and say Colo-*rah*-do and Nev-*ah*-da, which natives often don't.

Pinedale and Dubois were just as remote as Jackson itself, maybe more so, being even further from a railroad. There was the equally narrow and slippery road down from Yellowstone. Eventually a trickle of Model-T Fords from Kansas began to come in that way, "tin-can tourists," lowest of the low, scorned and hated by dudes, ranchers, and Jackson townspeople alike.

But despite Owen Wister's *Virginian*, Jackson (or was it "Jackson's"? – nobody seemed to be quite sure) Hole remained unknown except to upper-class Philadelphians, who have always felt they had a kind of absentee landlordship there, beginning with Wister, and a few other such from New York, Boston, and Chicago (nowhere much else, certainly, except for my father's friends from Princeton). Westerners had relations who came in for hunting and fishing. But the "damn carrot-eating farmers" from Idaho across the pass were Outsiders; the east of Wyoming, full of "damn woolies," was suspect, since the threat of an invasion of sheep was real and much feared, and the only metropolis within conception was Salt Lake, seat of The Church, almost three hundred miles away. Denver might as well have been on the moon.

It is hard to imagine just how much "ours" the northwest corner of this almost uninhabited valley was, or seemed to be. There were no ranches directly north of us at all, just the flats where our horses grazed, and the river. There was nothing between us and the Tetons except the rough track that straggled vaguely towards the dam and Sheffield's store and then pushed hardily but feebly on up to Yellowstone.

17

Two creeks ran between us and Menor's Ferry a few miles southward: Cottonwood and Spring. Along Cottonwood, there were a few old ranches like Ida Tarbell's girls' camp, the Half Moon. Miss Lucas had her hideaway among the aspens, guarded by fierce dogs.

Southward from the Ferry on each side of the river comparative civilization began, a string of ranches; but across the river from us spread empty flats again, sagebrush all the way to the Grovonts, sagebrush all the way north to the glacial break of Burnt Ridge. Beyond this were again hayfields, the Elk Ranch, the Triangle X, the Moosehead, a whole colony of long-settled ranches that made a quite separate subregion of its own up the Buffalo Fork towards Togwotee Pass.

Low down on the east side, creeping up from the city of Jackson was a farming settlement called Mormon Row, the furthest limit northward of the valley's early southward pioneering, the rural suburb of Jackson. Ranches ran up the Grovont River into the hills; but in fact you could have drawn a line across the middle of the valley at the Bar B C and another up and down the valley north and south through the midstream of the Snake, and in that northwest quarter there was nothing but scenery. The only exceptions were Sheffield's Camp and a few other cabins scattered off the empty wagon track up to the Yellowstone.

I like to say I was "the first white child born in the northwest quarter of Jackson Hole." There are probably other claimants—crazy Sargent up on the lake, I believe, sired children after he settled there and before I was born. Ben Sheffield's son also may have been born at the dam before I was, and others during the boom of the dam's construction. But I don't actually know of any; and of course prefer not to. Of this province of our Kingdom, in itself some forty miles long from

Menor's Ferry to Yellowstone Park, some twenty miles wide from the Snake River to Idaho, I definitely felt myself to be, if not king, certainly Heir Apparent. It was *my* country, *my* birthright. It certainly didn't seem to belong to anybody else.

2.

GOD'S COUNTRY AND MINE

IN later life my parents would embarrass and infuriate my adolescence by telling the story of how as a baby I once looked about me, thumped my fat chest, and proclaimed, "God and me made all this." Though somewhat of an exaggeration, it did rather give an inkling of the kinds of feelings my sister and I had about *our* country. If not actually in on the Creation, I certainly assumed myself to be an integral and original part of it. Like Adam and Eve, this garden had been planted for our benefit. That was the whole point of it. These were our mountains, and we gave them our names. These were our lakes, and we rode to them and swam in them at will. These were certainly our flats and benches, and above all this was our river. "Our" included parents and people like Joe, the foreman, who were essential parts of the scenery, like us. It might include a few well-liked wranglers. Dudes were allowed in as a special favor on our part. Tourists and strangers were not to be tolerated, despised on sight. The country belonged to God and us only.

This of course was in no sense a feeling of ownership or property. The very idea of "property" was alien to this conception of Eden, of untouched and, we forlornly hoped, untouchable wilderness. Since we were part of it, we didn't make

it any less virginal, less wild. But any outsider might con-
taminate.

Of course, the ranch did have bounds — the acres of my father's homestead claims. Buck fences, obligatory by the homestead law, marked these bounds, the edges of civilization; but
we had no real next-door neighbors. The south end of the
valley from the Ferry on down was of course no wilderness,
and hence not really part of God's Country. The town of Jackson was obviously the Devil's own. The east side of the river,
though wild, was so remote from us as to be almost mythical.
We never set foot over there, at least above the Ferry.

God's Country was that nearly empty northwest quarter that
included most of the best of the Tetons and the lakes and the
flats and the riverbed. Only Jackson Lake Dam, like Jackson
itself, represented evil, the Serpent, the evidence of the wick-
edness of the outside world, the spoilers and graspers and anti-
Christs of commercialism, the sign and symbol, realized as such
even then and even by us as children, of what could destroy
Eden if not stopped and controlled.

We were brought up on this, this was all part and parcel
of our vision of the Hole for as long as I can remember.
I could never, like some children, limit my identification to
a few square blocks or square miles of home territory. From
the beginning "my world" was half the size of Denmark, my
background was limited only by the mountains. And it was
always, from the beginning, a world obscurely threatened, a
world that could be violated again as it had once been violated by the dam.

Even to the eye of the dullest adult, the fundamental built-in
everyday glory of Jackson Hole is obvious and evident. The impact on a newborn child is almost inconceivable. Our recep-
tive parents at every moment encouraged our own receptive-

ness. The usual idyll of childish response to nature was compounded and made extravagant. Every item of the catalog of wonders, from curious yellow or black cobbles and odd-colored insects to peaks and storms and sunsets, had its special taste, flavor, meaning for us. It was exactly as though we did truly believe in beings, demigods, who lived in trees and rocks and places. These beings were beautiful and beneficent, but they were a bit scary too. Part of the wildness was fear; and a good thing. Dudes who weren't respectful, who ignored the taboos, could get into terrible trouble—and served them right. They were drowned in the river and fell off cliffs and bear and moose mauled them. You didn't fool around with these Presences. Respectful awe was the proper attitude, and you walked softly in Eden.

The most vivid of these presences were of course the animals, big and little: dark and fierce moose and bear, mysterious and elegant elk and deer. There was a lesser echelon of small game, coyotes rambling and howling all around us, porcupines padding and bristling, skunks that insisted on setting up house under the cabins of the Bar BC and unaccountably fighting each other with their own special weapons, thus making the cabins uninhabitable. Chiselers in their underground villages, otters along the streams, scuttling coneys up among the peaks, and efficient, stupid, talented beavers, so like their human counterparts—all these were part of the daily magic of our surroundings.

Most magical of all was the setting—the grand masculine Tetons, exhilarating but austere and aloof; the gentler, bosomy, feminine Grovonts that took the mellow evening light with an evocation of horn calls and lush Victorian hymns like "Now the day is over." Trees, conifers as dark and fierce as moose, aspens mysterious and elegant as deer, flowers in stained glass variety, multicolored collectable cobblestones, insects in air and water, the enormous sky full of stars, nowhere more brilliant than in Wyoming — these things about which I am still as excited as when I was a child, and almost as ignorant, could have been the introduction to an education in biology, botany, geology, or astronomy. I did have a spurt of adolescent enthusiasm for botany, but the formal education I had never touched any of this, or touched only to kill with a grammar of Latin names. The aesthetic still happily limps along, the scientific has withered away.

Quite aside from the west-side world of the Tetons and the east-side world of the Grovonts, yet right in the middle and almost too close for comfort, was the River. We heard its rushing by day and by night, we played in it, fished in it, and were enthralled and terrified by and of it.

One actual passage of diary, written already nostalgically at the age of twenty up on the Three Rivers (remembering a childhood now a vast ten years gone), does manage I still think (a vaster sixty years later) to convey some of the feeling that we had for our river when we lived at the Bar BC:

The river itself is a lot of the subconscious part of me. It's my first conception of "doom" — the swift gray-swirling water secretly eating the sagebrush flat away, in a curve of sliding, yellow cutbank. In my dreams it would wash the earth right out from under my feet. Sometimes at night I could actually hear the muffled rumble and crash, the thud of slipping earth. In other dreams I would lose myself in dense, sandy islands of cottonwood and alder. Through a green, vibrating noon I would go lost beside a stagnant reach, yellow with monkey flower, and call and call — and Mammy wouldn't be there.

But the river was also adventure and mystery. There were places where the firs grew hanging over the oily, gurgling curves of water — deep, slow currents, the epitome of danger. There might be moose

23

in there, anything in those bushy thickets. The fisherman's ford across the main stream was from a riverside grove of cottonwoods called the Picnic Ground. We usually played in a spot right below it. We went down the cutbank and jumped across a little pebbly stream to a big sandbar. How many cities and towers and great engineering works were built there!

If you crossed the river at the Picnic Ground, in low water, you went across to the big, dark island. I would wade with Daddy when he went fishing, sliding my big rubber boots along the slippery bottom so I wouldn't fall. There were tramps through dark places, groves of fir, enormous willows, or along beaches and dry rock beds and shallow riffles. There would be a long time of sitting, building with cobbles or sand while Daddy cast, and then the excitement when he caught something and I ran to him with the net. Sometimes he'd inspect the line of boxes, the "ripraps," great frames of logs filled with cobbles, set to direct the current away from the bank on Bar BC land. The worst cutaways were just below the Picnic Ground, and then also on the road to the Ferry, where old road tracks, a terrible sight, plunged out into nothingness over the edge.

We were always very proud of our doom, the river, and there was a story of a cabin whose land washed from under it one night with all the people in it, a story we believed and cherished and told everyone. It was always there, our river, always in our thoughts whether we looked across it to the far, familiar shapes of the four o'clock golden Grovonts; or when we saw it from the edge of Timber Island, wriggling up to the unknown north and down to the settled south; or as we came off the first bench, tired, with our hands full of magnificent stones, and we would take in again with familiar fondness how our river sucked in towards the panorama of the ranch — roofs of cabins, the pool, the groves of fir, the aspens — curved beside them in a line of white riverbed, pale glistening water, green, dark lines of spruce.

And above all at night when the murmur would grow as the darkness fell unnoticed before supper, when bells rang and the horses clattered up the bench and everyone came along the paths through flowers to supper, then striking one suddenly again with its quietness when the evening was over, and the door of the convivial lampwarm cabin closed us into the bare night, that night so very high and motionless and crystal cold, held in the long singing of the river.

Then at last, in the room, when the lamp was blown out and we went quickly over the chilly floor to bed — through the window, paler than the blackness of the room, would come the long ceaseless sh-h-h from the riverbed, full of secret rustlings, pulses, whispers, more still even than the night silence.

The two other lesser rivers were also part of our childhood: rough, boyish, boisterous Cottonwood Creek, outlet of Jenny Lake, dangerous to cross in spring; and smooth, secretive, girlish Spring Creek, that oozed out mysteriously from under the first bench.

Each one of the lakes at the foot of the Tetons also had a personality. Jenny was brash and beautiful and obvious, rather like its name. Bradley and Leigh were remote and hidden from us by distances of forest. Phelps belonged to the JY and was never "ours." Ours was Taggart. This was the lake we liked best. We rode there all the time and swam in it naked. A fine, flat, gray granite rock jutting right into the water where the trail ended made a wonderful sunbathing terrace after the delicious sun-rippling dips in the lake itself. Nobody came to disturb us. People always came to round-eyed deep blue Jenny. Even then it had a sort of public character. Pale green Taggart was private, our own Wagnerian-peak–dominated ol' swimmin' hole.

Of all the waters the most intimate, most loved, most truly our own were the ditches. Ditches were of course man-made, domestic. Ditches, though they were so much like streams, differed from nature as horses differed from elk or dogs from coyotes. With the help of some expert my father had laid out our ditch for several miles across the flat from a point far up on Cottonwood Creek. To this day a long line of by now sizable willows and alders and cottonwoods goes around the south end of Timber Island and out across the sagebrush to the Bar BC. The ditches were our salvation, the thing that made life possible, water in the desert. For, despite all the water around us in river and creek, we couldn't have really lived on the ranch without the water from that ditch.

It came down the first bench in a pipe, a "flume," into a big laundry shed. From there the main stream ran southward through the ranch and split into two channels. One went east to form the swimming pool, and then ran off through the field into the river. The other passed through the corral area, watered a big vegetable garden, and then passed back across by the cabins to rejoin the swimming pool. There were, of course, wells from which we got our actual drinking and washing water. The principal well stood in that L-shaped front area of the main cabin where I once stood lost in the snow in my first memories.

We played in the Snake, we played in Spring Creek, but above all we played in the ditches. From infancy to adolescence we sailed boats and made dams, built riverside cities of cobblestone, dug side canals and constructed "waterworks" along them. And with the ditches came the invading host of water creatures: five-legged skates that skimmed the gelatinous tension of water's surface while the sun reflected their four-leaf-clover shadows on the ditch-bottom shallows, ringed all around the edges by gold. Numberless tadpoles turned into numberless tiny frogs. Kindly, elegant little water snakes wriggled away from us, sticking out their harmless forked pink tongues. Minnows went down the rippling bright current to shoal in the wide swimming pool, the pool where we learned to swim, held up by breath-inflated white canvas water wings. This was the pool where ladies dipped themselves, dressed, to my earliest eyes, in rubber shoes, black stockings, floppy black bathing dresses (you couldn't call them "suits") reaching to the knees, and floppy mob caps over all that put-up hair. When they swam, the ladies used a stately breast stroke.

Men wore either long one-piece suits with hips shielded by a discreet extra skirt of wool, or, later on, the universal blue flannel shorts with white canvas belt and white jersey topshirt. Our wranglers, like most Western horsemen, scorned the water and never came near the pool.

All of our life that was not devoted to horses and animals, people and indoor playing, books and dreams, was devoted to these water places: the river, the creeks, the ditches, the pool. It was impossible not to sense the oddnesses and importances of water in this country. Water did not come in the air, from the sky. Water was a special gift of the mountains and their perpetual snow. Unlike the East, where humidity and dampness were of the essence, the West was essentially a desert. The wonderful brilliance of the sky and of the air was that of desert sky and air. It was only because we were so high and that our winters collected so much snow that we had any trees or flowers or water to drink in summer. The summer rains would never do, sudden brief thunderstorms on July afternoons that sometimes failed to lay the dust, making splattered patterns that dried immediately. There were a few three-day rainy spells in August, grateful but only temporary relief, or a snowstorm in early September, sometimes a day or two of slush that marked the end of summer and the beginning of what should be the long, glorious, clear Indian Summer of September and October.

Every summer was in fact a drought, and only the life-giving flow of melting snow from the mountain glaciers, only our man-made rippling ditches, or our reechoing wells (probably just seepage of the ditch traveling underground through the cobblestones) kept us alive from the solid spring rains of June till the first November blizzards. How thick and deep the dust would get in August! Team horses, with little curtains of fringe hung over their noses against flies, would plod down the road through the ranch from gate to gate, bent on ranch business, and stirring up great wheel-sifted clouds of it.

We never felt that our ditches, our fences, our cabins were in any way a violation of the surrounding wilderness. They fitted. The ranch was the natural focus of Our Country, the necessary complement, the human nest that justified the grandeur about us. For without us, without Adam and Eve to appreciate Eden, what was the point of it?

On that final bottom-third level of the flats, below mountains, below low moraine foothills and the two benches, on the sagebrush level gnawed by the curve of the river, were strung out the ranch buildings. They were nearly all of unpeeled logs, though a few were of boards. The logs were set up crisscross like notched match sticks, sometimes carefully finished off to make neat, square corners. The cabins stood a few feet off the dirt on concrete supports, the walls hardly higher than a man. The roofs had a very low pitch, the length of the roof supported by long logs, the roof itself of boards. On a few of the older cabins, following a pioneer tradition, the roofs were covered with sod. Wild flowers grew up there in summer and it was pretty, but the dirt had a way of leaking down during wetness. Most of the cabins had ordinary tar-paper covering, not elegant but practical. Shingles were a fancy introduction of the 1930s.

The cracks between the logs of the walls were filled in by chinking—rough cement of river gravel and lime held in place at the bottom by willow wands. This chinking was always coming out and having to be replaced. Doors and windows, like the tar-paper roofing, were store bought, or at least made along with the roof boards in local saw mills, not on the ranch itself. Otherwise cabins were built entirely by men on the ranch out of material from the ranch.

The windows were always "lazy," put in so that they opened sideways, not up and down, thus saving any necessity for sash weights. They were placed high so that they would be above all but the very deepest snows. These lazy windows are the chief charm and most characteristic feature of the western log cabin, convenient and pretty and indigenous. But cabins always seem rather dark by daylight.

The more important cabins had fireplaces, rude affairs made of cemented cobblestones. They too were built entirely by local hands out of local materials. Like the chinking, these cobbles had a way of falling out. In deep winter fireplaces had to be closed in. Real heat was always achieved by wood-burning tin stoves with their shiny, black tin chimneys going up through the roof. Big green aspen logs would be inserted just before bedtime, and the stove shut tight, both dampers closed; then my father would hop up at dawn, open the dampers, and rush back to bed as the long-smouldering logs burst into a roaring blaze that would make the room cozily warm for dressing.

There was no plumbing of course. White enamel tin pitchers and wash basins, with blue edges, did for hands and face. Big, round, silvery galvanized tubs washed bodies and clothes, the latter with the help of wood-and-tin washboards. Baths were elaborate once-a-week businesses: a bucket of cold water from the well, another bucket heated on the stove top, then the steaming hot water rattling into the round tub with its own peculiar soft splashing sound and tinny-steamy smell, enough cold water to make the bath bearable, and then, especially for a child, the delicious scrunched-up water-messiness of the bath itself, splashing soapsuds for yards roundabout. Nothing made you feel cleaner. Then the heavy tub with its dirty gray water had to be dragged out and emptied off the edge of the porch onto the ground.

Outhouses, discreetly and often rather lonesomely hidden in the willows, were universal. White enameled chamber ~ots with lids and handles might serve for indoor emergencies, but even at 50° below outhouses were the rule, and my mother's bitterest memories of her winters out West involved trudging out to these unheated and unheatable edifices through five feet of snow. How did she stand it? In summer they were delightful, kept scrupulously clean, with a Sears Roebuck catalog for reading and for emergency paper. Flies and bees buzzed lazily about, and there was a strong antiseptic smell of lye to be dusted from cans down the holes into that nasty cloacal mess.

When the dude ranch was in full swing, an old white-moustached gentleman called Johnny Van Vliet tended to water delivery, going around each morning and evening with a barrel on wheels, full of hot water. Every cabin had its own set of buckets, wash basin and pitcher, chamber pot. Johnny was the "roustabout" and carried ranch gossip around with his water and wood. If extra water was needed in between by our family, we children dipped it from the ditch.

Lighting was by kerosene lamps and candles. When you went into a dark cabin coming back from supper at the main cabin, you lit a big kitchen match and then with it a candle. There was something about this ritual that had powerful associations — the sharp sulphur smell of the match, the soft, eerie, wavering light of the candle on the variegated log walls. Then you lit the lamp, taking off the shade from its delicate brackets;

taking off the fragile, tall glass chimney that bellied out at wick level; lighting and then adjusting the wick; placing chimney and shade back on their fragile supports. Part of the process was the act of sloshing the aluminum base about before lighting and listening to the sound to be sure there was enough kerosene inside.

Candles were friendly and fascinating, but kerosene lamps were always a menace. If you put the crescent-shaped flame too high, the chimney would soot up or even crack. If you were foolish enough to touch a hot chimney, you got nasty blisters on your fingers. It was always such a nuisance getting the chimneys back into those damn clips and the shades back over the chimneys onto those precarious brackets. Lamps had to be filled regularly and the chimneys polished and the wicks, like strips of canvas belt, trimmed. Chimneys were always cracking and breaking, glass all over the place, no immediately available replacement, lamp unusable for that evening, and so forth. Even when you had light, it was never really good for reading. The kerosene lamp, in fact, was a fine example of the disadvantages of semicivilization, the awkward halfway house between true craft and true technology, far more unpleasant than primitive candles, far more inconvenient than electricity. I always feel nostalgia for the candle, but not the kerosene lamp, cozy though it could be when in proper operation. Yet how violently I resented the coming of electricity!

The ranch itself was, I suppose, a sort of cultural halfway house, but a happy and successful one. It was not part of the great web of integrated civilization, tied to unknown, faraway, mysterious factories and power plants by electric wires; and yet it was not entirely self-supporting, a homestead like those of the eighteenth century based on the innumerable crafts of weaving, spinning, carding, carpentry, food raising. There was no candle dipping or soapmaking on the Bar BC, few of those hand skills that settled America and kept it going for its first vigorous two hundred years. We did not, in fact, make anything. Our candles, our doors and windows, our nails, straps and ropes, our saddles and stoves and lamps were all store-bought, or, more likely, bought out of mail-order catalogs. For between us and technological civilization passed the invisible link of the post office. Everything came, or could come, from Sears Roebuck and Montgomery Ward—fishing boots, guitars, phonograph records, Bibles, lace curtains, milk separators. The only crafts used were carpentry (in the building and repair of cabins, outhouses, fences) and the ordinary skills of blacksmithing and horseshoeing.

More skilled and more special was the creation of furniture. Almost all the furniture on the ranch was built on the place, some of it marvelously eccentric—chairs of moose horn, tables of beautifully polished aspen wood.

As for our clothes, they too were all store-bought, made in San Francisco by Levi Strauss (pants), or Philadelphia by Stetson (hats), or Pendleton, Oregon (woolen shirts and pants). Our Levis, incidentally, were never called "jeans" but "overalls." The correct name in those days was "waist overalls" to distinguish them from baggy painter's overalls. Hats were "sombreros."

A great deal of our food came out of cans, but we did have a large vegetable garden where, during the very short and late season, we got some of our salads, carrots, cabbages, peas—all with great labor and in scanty quantity. We had chickens and their eggs, we had pigs to eat and garbage to be eaten. Beef was local, and we got a good deal of random game meat during the year, mostly elk (as a baby, I had elk blood mixed with my milk). Fish depended on the skill of whatever fishermen were present. We had, of course, our own cows and their milk. Meat and milk were kept in the high, cool, concrete-floored meat-and-ice house, kept fresh by melting ice, cut in winter from the swimming pool, embalmed in summer in sawdust. Shopping in earlier days was pretty arduous, but later on automobiles made Jackson more easily available.

There were no paved roads until the thirties. Originally there were only tracks through the sagebrush or lumber roads through the woods. Later on, another miserable "halfway house" consisted of scraped gravel roads, full of enormous cobbles that bounced and banged against running boards and sometimes broke engines. My earliest memories of travel were by team and buckboard. Then, somewhere in the earliest twenties, came the truck.

The truck was a big, rickety, high-pants White; the first one had gas headlights that had to be lighted by hand like our reading lamps. It was for years the only automobile on the ranch. Dudes were brought in and taken out by it, and the sound of its hoarse, brazen Klaxon coming down the bench at evening, announcing arrivals, was a high point of any day. One of these early trucks seemed to have no doors by the front seat.[1] This incredibly casual arrangement, which presumed that one never went much faster than twenty miles an hour, true enough on the roads of the time, almost killed me. We were in Yellowstone. The truck swung up the carriage drive of the Lake Hotel. I was spun out of the front seat and rolled down the gravel roadway. I was bundled in a big, burly, black sweater, which saved me from bruises and made all the tourists think I was a bear cub. I got up unhurt and much

[1] See illustration.

gratified by the ring of disappointed curiosity about me when I undoubled.

Life on the ranch was governed by the bell, swinging up on its tall log pole. I longed for the rare privilege of being allowed to ring it. There was one kitchen but two dining rooms and sets of meals: one for the outfit on a long oilcloth-covered table, with breakfast at dawn of coffee and many huge flapjacks, and another more elegant dining room for the dudes with smaller tables. The universal setup of all dude ranches prevailed: everyone had their own sleeping cabins, but everyone ate together at the main cabin (cabins, not cottages; main cabin, not lodge—those silly dudes were always making such ludicrous mistakes).

Breakfast was delightful and haphazard. People came irregularly; there was always the fun of those who came just before the deadline—or just after. In later years there was a so-called store where latecomers could pay to get a late breakfast. Lunch and dinner were more formal and everyone was supposed to come together and on time between the first and second bells. The tables held half a dozen, and this caused excruciating social problems. Who was to sit with whom? Fortunate the family big enough to take up a whole table. When we were little we had early, separate dinner, eating with whatever other small children were on the ranch. There were the usual refusals to eat spinach and jello. Spinach had such a horrid look, slimy. Jello quivered. No troubles at all with white-iced, diamond-shaped sections of cake cut from a big flat pan.

The principal occupation of the ranch and of its dudes was riding. As compared with other ranches, the riding at the Bar BC suffered from disadvantages. To get to any real scenery in the Tetons, you had to cross several miles of flats, which could be excruciatingly hot and dusty. Other rides went up and down the river, but were not very interesting. That did not seem to bother anybody, however, and at least the flats provided splendid opportunities for fast riding. "Galloping endlessly over the prairies" was our sarcastic catchphrase for what most of the younger dudes seemed to think riding was meant to be. We, of course, knew better. The really useful gait of a horse was an endless fast walk, varied by a gentle jog or a gentle lope (but never over cobblestones or up and down rises). A run was useful in emergencies. A trot was "dudish."

To take care of all this riding there was a complex of constructions. There were two big corrals, a long low saddle shed (never "tack room") open on one side with all the saddles up on numbered racks, a hitching fence opposite the saddle shed, and back beyond all this the barn and blacksmith shop. The whole riding operation was in the charge of our foreman, Joe Lepage, along with all the rest of the ranch activities, except those of kitchen and dining room and cabin cleaning. These were taken care of by a housekeeper responsible to my mother. Under Joe were one or two guides, who spent most of the summer out in the hills pack tripping. The daily routine was handled by the wranglers who rounded up the horses every morning from their range up on the flats, caught and saddled the dude horses, and took parties out riding.

Every day you signed up for riding in a corral book kept in a small room of the main cabin that served as entrance hall, writing room, and mail depot. The more experienced dudes went out on their own, but preferably never alone. My parents or Joe took out the very inexperienced. My sister and I guided children of our own age. But most of the time we went by ourselves.

Horse adventures and horse peculiarities took up a great

deal of the time and interest and conversation on the ranch. Both dudes and horses were unpredictable and ornery. Fat ladies were hoisted up on groaning horses and then refused to get off. "How do you make it go?" terrified neophytes would quaver, clutching the pommel or holding the reins in two hands agape to each side. One woman actually got up on the wrong side, found herself facing backwards, but insisted on being led out riding that way.

The ultimate shame of course was to be led. As very little children, our tiny legs sticking straight like handles, mounted on some huge, docile old horse (a black horse usually called Joe seems to be standard equipment on any well-organized ranch; on the Bar BC his name was Just So), we would be led around the ranch. Later on, of course, we had our own horses, and I had my own spurs and my own little angora chaps, black and white and shaggy. Pride could mount no higher.

The other great occupation was fishing. The Snake River was world famous for its fishing in those underpopulated days, and many of the dudes spent their time by the water and never even looked at a horse. Henry van Dyke—essayist, poet, clergyman (then so famous), dean of American letters and fishermen—condescended to fish our river. Old snapshots show Henry and my father holding a long line of huge trout sagging between them. By "fishing" we meant fly fishing. Worms or grasshoppers were forbidden to anybody except children. My father was indefatigable, and I went out on innumerable trips with him. I enjoyed the trips, but he never was able to make a fisherman of me. I couldn't stand all that gear, the fussy business of tying on flies, the lines that got tangled up in the willows.

The big interruptions to the ranch-bound routine of riding and fishing were pack trips, short jaunts into the Tetons, preferably up Death Canyon, or longer trips of one or two weeks eastwards into the Grovonts and Absorakas. Social life — consisting either of little dances and picnics within the company of the ranch itself, or larger sprees involving the other dude ranches — also broke up ordinary life. The climax of the season was the rodeo in Jackson. During my infancy my parents would go to local dances, particularly in winter, riding for half a day to get there and then riding back by dawn. Babies were brought to these dances and laid out in rows, facilitating the kind of practical joke described by Wister where the babies could be mixed up and taken back to the wrong home without anyone's knowing the difference.

I don't remember any of such occasions myself, but I do certainly remember the Fancy Dress Balls at the Bar BC, White Grass, and JY. These were annual affairs too, like the rodeo. Costumes were, of course, long on ingenuity and short on materials, relying heavily on sheets, towels, and animal rugs. They represented two weeks of hard labor. Music was by hand-cranked Victrola or amateur talent, the belle of the ball was usually the most glamorous cabin girl, draped casually in a coyote skin.

The wranglers refused to get into costume, going no further than a cork moustache; but their regular Saturday-night getups were costume enough with fancy boots decorated with steerheads and butterflies, great gold and silver belt buckles, tight custom-made riders, and shirts of indescribably vivacious color and design. Part of the costume of those days was a loose neckerchief, also wildly colorful, and always a big hat, worn on all occasions.

I have a medley of memories of these occasions through the years, at the Bar BC or up at the JY. My costumes generally went in for humor, not beauty. They were usually very uncomfortable. My parents did me up when a little tyke as the Fish Footman from *Alice*, with a great cardboard head that made it impossible for me to see or do anything. My mother once went as a mermaid, all wrapped up so that she couldn't walk. Much later on, I remember going to the JY as a "dead secret," swathed in a sheet and twined about with black typewriter ribbon, effective perhaps but again totally inhibiting.

A description in a diary entry of one of the last of these affairs at the JY, of a much later period and based for me not on the Bar BC but the Three Rivers, does, nonetheless, give the general picture. August 21, 1931:

Got into my costume for the JY fancy dress ball. Dressed as a "Salacian Peasant"—black shirt, vest, bucking belt, bag over my head in an attempt to look like a sort of Russian. Julie also dressed as a Salacian, very pretty indeed. We left rather early, without Ma. Went to the Fabian's for supper. Rainstorm coming up over the Tetons, very black but not hiding the mountains. Sang Salacian songs all the way. Finally left for the JY, singing "Prairie Flower" and "Looking Through the knot-hole in Grandpa's wooden leg." We got there already hilarious. Bar BC -ites: Irv (Corse) dressed as Angela (he shaved off his moustache to do it) and Angela dressed as Irv. Very funny. He looked awful, and she looked like a little old man of seventy. Anne Young dressed in a Russian sort of costume with deep blue velvet pants. George, Ced, H. H., Priscilla, and Helen Page, she in pajamas very pretty. Girl dressed as a bundle. She couldn't move or walk or hardly even see. Some man in a very strange costume, long, wide, green-white-red stripes and a horse collar over his head so that it stuck out in front. Any girl who danced with him had to stick her head inside it. The Reeds arrived, Dizzy in her chaps, vest, and the Indian warbonnet, all bead and buckskin and very stunning. George also in a Russian costume, more or less. Danced and danced. Fabian girl, Anne

Young, Julie, Priscilla, and Helen, etc. Ted Dominick dressed as some old Yukon trapper in all the old junk from the Bar BC store. The dancing got wilder and wilder. Disorganized Paul Jones (commanded by the "gigolo"). Everybody joined hands and ran around as fast as possible in wiggles. Drunk and disgusting old man, etc. The horse-collar man got drunk. He said he was a Princeton graduate and kept telling Daddy not to get discouraged. "Just keep it up, Struthers. People are beginning to notice you." Lots of stomping and careering around as the time went on. Running up and down the room whooping and yelling. Ted Dominick and Betty Laidlaw fell down with a great crash. We left about 2, while the party was still going strong. Got home about 4. Heavy frost. Bed. Slept till 10:30.

Since, as of 1931, my father had been on the best-seller list for months with *Festival*, the horse-collar man's encouragement was rather superfluous.

A much more serious holiday was the annual rodeo in Jackson. This was the climax of the summer season, and, if we never went to Jackson at any other time, we always went there then. The younger and more irresponsible and daring hands competed, got drunk, had fights in bars. The adult dudes got drunk, usually from the base of a tourist-camp cabin nicknamed the Ritz. The Burt family often spent the night at the Crabtree Hotel, eating our meals boardinghouse style at the long tables decorated with racks of condiments.

The rodeo events — roping, racing, bucking horses, bulldogging — were pretty amateurish and full of long, dusty delays; but nearly everybody who entered was somebody we knew, somebody who worked for us or worked for somebody we knew. We were fiercely partisan, rooting for our boys. Even our dudes entered things like bareback riding or races. I remember, from a later period of the Bar BC, Dewey Dominick riding a bareback horse with matches in his back pocket. The

friction ignited them and he left a splendid trail of smoke behind him, like a jet plane. Riders were thrown and maimed,
and there was a good deal of suspense and drama involved;
but mostly it was a time of sitting on the bare-board stands,
or milling about town aimlessly. The grownups met their
friends, and my father stood about talking endlessly and endlessly with his cronies while we waited and waited and waited.
O God, how many hot hours we all waited for Dad in Jackson,
at rodeos or any other time.

Later on, as an adolescent, my own participation in the
festivities was more active; as a child the rodeo was just one
big blurry event, an excitement compounded of the novelty
of being off the ranch and a good deal of thirsty boredom.
Later on I got more involved, and various diary entries recon-
struct some of the simple, rackety doings.

In 1930, for instance, we watched the show not from the
stands but from cars parked along the back of the grounds. I
won a silver dollar at roulette, and we decided to spend the
night at the Crabtree Hotel in a huge bridal-suite room with
a grand piano, leopard skin couch, and so forth. This was for
the parents. I myself ended up in "room no. 8 with Cal Carrington." A movie with Marion Davies in it filled up time
before dancing. Where the dancing took place was not speci-
fied, but en route I fell down and "skinned myself all up."
"Big fight outside of booze den next to Maggie's hot dog stand
while we were there getting hot dogs. . . . Roosevelt boy now
looks like a dope fiend." The "Roosevelt boy" was Franklin
D. Roosevelt's son Elliott who was working for the J O, a boys'
camp run as an adjunct to the Bar BC. He was presumably
not involved in the fight himself, but just among those present.

In 1931 there seemed to have been two rodeos. The first

one was on July 26. We went straight to Ma Reed's for lunch, then to the show:

Clouds, dust, yells, threats of rain, the aeroplane behind us and the grandstand making a fearful racket. "Rodeo handkerchiefs, take your pick and leave the rest, your choice is mine" sold by the supposed blind man with the disagreeable face. Bucking, bulldogging, calf roping. Homer the clown and a lady bronc twister. A girl trick rider, the blond trick roper, Old Man Scott and his trained dog. Races—regular, chariot, Roman. The calf roping and bulldogging were best. Record calf roping, 13½ seconds! Nobody hurt. Altogether pretty good. Sorry to see so many little felt hats in the audience (i.e., as opposed to proper western sombreros).

Afterwards night life began with another meal at Ma Reed's.

Then visited the different gambling halls (3) and altogether lost about $1.50 by the time I got through. Then we all went to the dance. Quite dark by then. It's very elegant, the new dance hall. Tricky lights and a floor painted like a checkerboard. All log, and quite nice. Lots of Jackson youths in big pants and sport shoes. [Again, not western.] Rather sad looking. Home late. Kept falling asleep in the car and waking up very cold. Bed sure felt good.

The other rodeo in the fall kept us busy for two days. On September 2 we had lunch at the more modern Blue Bird Cafe, where were "the Woodwards en masse. Story of Phil Dechert having written a list of 'queer people I have met' beginning with John Dodge and ending with Dr. Woodward. Charlie Woodward saw it. John Dodge came in and talked for a while. Quite pitiful." John Dodge was a very eccentric Eastern remittance man who led a peculiar, ragged, bachelor life and drove a pair of famous, refractory mules. The Woodwards were early Bar B C dudes. "Went to Rodeo. Very few

41

people. Not much of a show, but fun because we knew everyone in it. Decided to go home and have our fling tomorrow."

The next day the show seemed to be exciting, since many friends were involved: "Howard Henry and Forrest thrown but not badly hurt; Bill also, but not hurt. Meeks won first money, Cecil Jackson second. Fraser rode bareback but didn't receive much competition and stayed on. Stagecoach race, Helen Page, Ora Wood in yellow, Jim W. and Sarah Gardner in red as passengers, the damn fools."

Afterwards:

Went to Jesse's [Worts] but no roulette wheel. Eventually wandered down to the "Ritz." It was in one of the little cement cabins in the Ideal Lodge. Glen Ferrin, Harvey Ferrin, Priscilla Page, Jim Collins, Daddy, Si Ferrin, and Bisphams and K. Reed came in. Much talk and merriment, especially between Dutch Hawkins, Si, and Dad. People coming in and out all the time. Bill Fuller the bartender. Finally left. Jesse's again. The roulette wheel having disappeared last night in the raid, I mastered the mysteries of craps; enough to lose everything but 75 cents. Supper at the Log Cabin. Joined in Jim Collins's party, Reeds and Corses. Returned to Jesse's, got the dice in the crap game. Won $3.00, just enough to tide me over for the evening.

From that time on it seems to have been all downhill — a movie, *The Great Meadows* with "trite situations"; a dispiriting dance; and then going home complicated by my father's having had too much merriment at the Ritz and being in no condition to drive. Like many such, he insisted on driving; but we all got back safely.

The disappearance of the roulette wheel in midrodeo was typical of the peculiar law enforcement of state and county. Gambling was and still is illegal, but flourished; however, the laws were liable to be temporarily and suddenly enforced for very odd reasons. This may have inhibited roulette but certainly did not stop gambling. "Bright moon. Sleep till about twelve." So ended another rodeo.

Amusements on the ranch itself were somewhat milder. There was a tremendous amount of cardplaying and horseplay, general roughhousing, impromptu baseball games, peculiar versions of polo, one of them played with brooms on the field out back of the main cabin. Poker was the big game, and grownups won or lost a good deal of money at it, not so different from Jackson gambling in that respect. I learned auction bridge at an early age, and I was something of an infantile expert. I reached my height at about twelve. Then contract came in and I failed to keep up with the times. Mah-jongg loomed large in the twenties, to my father's disgust. He found it inappropriate to Wyoming. I loved the sets and played with stray pieces. Where are they all now, those winds and dragons?

But unquestionably our principal extracurricular activity was music. The one significant intrusion of civilization, besides the mail-order catalog, was the record player or "Victrola" (always that, not "gramaphone"). This was of course hand cranked, like the White truck. Its stack of already outmoded records, red- or black-labeled Victor, blue Columbia, brown Brunswick, included my sentimental favorites, "Alice Blue Gown" and "My Isle of Golden Dreams." This latter meant much more to me than it had any business to, conjuring up not Hawaii but an imaginary paradise worthy of the most fantastic nineteenth-century painter with red-orange, misty, mountain waterfalls. There were tinny, tinkly old jazz tunes, with lots of clippity-clop and banjo strumming. There was jaunty Sir Harry Lauder, of whose dialect I could make no sense at all.

Much more indigenous was our own music making. The ranch invariably supported one or two good guitar players, from Adolph Borie and my Aunt Jean Burt; Felicia Gisycka, the Countess's daughter, who gave us children private recitals; Marion Danforth, a smart single lady who had a repertory of quaint Edwardian music-hall ditties like "Gilbert, the Filbert, the Colonel of the Nuts" and "In der vintertime, in der valley green"; right down to performers of my last years on the Bar BC, such as Curt Winsor and Doc Andrus. Curt still has a complete collection of all these songs, which it is to be hoped will be carefully preserved.

Whole evenings were spent by the fire or outdoors on benches along the log walls of the main cabin, with or without guitar, listening to songs or singing ourselves. The guitar and singing-session repertory was varied and eclectic, but the chief staple was "cowboy songs." These varied between genuine folk songs and made-up imitations. My father's favorites, "Ten Thousand Cattle," "So Bossy So," and "The Chisholm Trail," illustrated the range. "Ten Thousand Cattle," for instance, had been written by Owen Wister himself to be sung by Trampas, the villain in the stage version of *The Virginian*. I have always suspected "So Bossy So" of a sophisticated origin, but there was no doubt about the folkishness of "The Chisholm Trail" and its innumerable verses. On these Westerns, real and imitation, I was suckled, and though I never learned to play the guitar, I certainly learned to sing a lot of them.

The apex of my career as a singer of western ballads occurred in the 1950s. I was a Fellow one summer at the Breadloaf Conference, in Vermont, where guitar playing and folk singing were also much in evidence. On one occasion when Robert Frost was presiding deity at an after-dinner get-together, and singing was going on, it somehow got through to him that I had cowboy songs on tap. He insisted on my sitting right up in front of his face, not three feet away, and going through my repertoire. The guitarist, Lincoln Barnett, who was supposed to sort of improvise along with me, gave up, so I had to proceed through song after song — "Old Paint," "Spanish Is a Loving Tongue," "I have no use for the women" — very much solo. "Go on, go on!!" Frost would croak, after each number, a tribute not to my singing but to his interest in the material. I never before or since participated in a more excruciating command performance.

One of our wranglers, Hugh Emery, though almost totally tone deaf, had a store of extremely genuine songs that he sang (so to speak) as we rode along. In a dreary monotone, not inappropriate sometimes, he taught me "I have no use for the women," a favorite with both of us. We especially relished that dying fall at the end: "And many a similar puncher/as he passes that mou-und of stones/thinks of some similar woman/and en-vies them mo-o-ouldering bo-o-ones." Another of his, as I remember, was the jauntier "Way up high in the Sirey Peaks."

I also associate with Hugh, though I can never be sure just when and from whom I really did hear most of these songs, such basic ballads as the lugubrious "Little Joe, the Wrangler" ("He'll wrangle never more/His days with the remuda they are o'er.") and "When the work's all done this fall" ("He opened wide his *blue* eyes, and looking all around/he mentioned *to* his com-*rades* to sit down on the ground."). The more really touching and musical songs like "Colorado Trail" and the true and proper modal tune of "Bury Me not on the Lone Prairie" have a somewhat less authentic atmosphere; in any case, Hugh never sang these. "Eyes like the morning star/cheeks like the rose/Laura was a pretty girl/God almighty knows." Obviously

45

not long for this world, that Laura. As for the "Cowboy's La-ment," nothing evokes the wide-open spaces more nostalgically than that dirge—with the *right* modal tune.

One of my very earliest song memories was the lullaby "My uncle he lives on the flat/and the banner he waves is a broad brim hat/He doesn't ride fast and he doesn't ride slow/He's the goldarn [children's version] best cowboy in the rodey-ee-o./Hush-a-by-baby/punch-a-buckaroo/Daddy'll be home when the round-up is through." I don't know where this song came from. When did anyone last use the term "buckaroo"? My parents sang it to me as a sure-enough lullaby; I never knew anybody else who had ever heard of it or sung it.[2] My father printed it in the *Diary of a Dude Wrangler*, but used "platte" instead of "flat" in the first line. I remember it as "flat."

Mixed up in all this there were of course always meretri-cious commercial items like "Rag Time Cowboy Joe" or "In the Gloaming of Wyoming." Whatever happened to "gloam-ings"? Like buckaroos, they have vanished away. We tended to scorn such obvious confections, and even such semicivilized artifacts as "Home on the Range" were considered pretty low.

But there was also a great mixed bag of non-Western songs that we were brought up on—pre–World War I English music-hall songs like "Knocked 'em in the Old Kent Road" or "Granny was a quaint old bird" ("the things she did were most absurd./She would walk out for miles with the cats on the tiles." A doubly mysterious evocation to me since I had no idea what "tiles" could be). There were Irish ballads like "Where the mountains of Morna go down to the sea" and the wonderful "Spanish Lady."

---

[2] The Abbott Moffatt family, early Bar BC dudes, now of Princeton, New Jersey, still remember and sing this song and those of my Aunt Jean to children and grandchildren.

Hours and hours of singing and listening in the pearly warm twilight, in the dark fire-rustling cabin-cave, built up associations for me towards this international anthology that mixed the crudest sort of commercial pop of the teens, a real indigenous living local folk tradition, and a sophisticated taste for the exotic. Some of the Western songs dated back to the days of cattle drives, like "The Chisolm Trail." Some of them were brand new, like the perhaps semisynthetic or at least composed "Sirey Peaks" with its references to Prohibition ("For them was the days when a good cowpoke/could oil up his insides."). It was with this sort of thing that Aunt Jean temporarily bewitched Francis Biddle during the long snowbound winter, and which she tried to imitate in her own songs.

We sat around on benches in the front L of the main cabin and watched the Tetons grow to sharp-notched silhouettes and barbershopped "Aura Lee" and "Working on the Railroad" in close harmony. In the evening, by the moonlight or in the gloaming, I could hear the banjos ringing, or the Victrola twanging from the outfit's get-togethers in a cabin across the vegetable garden from ours—popular tunes, not Western ones or folk songs, full of the mysterious excitement of grown-up goings on, love affairs, and echoes of the great world. Never since have I had a richer romantic effect from far-away summer-evening music.

Later on we danced informally to the Victrola in a special so-called dance cabin constructed on the other side of the swimming pool in the later twenties. There smart matrons like Mrs. Frew and her sister Mrs. Dilworth, of Pittsburgh, practiced the Black Bottom, and of an evening we small-fry hopped about to "Hallellujah" and slithered to "Limehouse Blues."

Higher things sometimes intruded. A group of Bryn Mawr

girls put on a sort of fairy pageant accompanied by a record of Maurice Ravel's "Jeux d'eaux." Somehow Bryn Mawr pixies did not fit in with Wyoming. I was always composing pieces on the dance-cabin piano with titles like "Aspens." Professionals sometimes entertained us, like the egregious Powder River Jack and his Kitty, all in the most synthetic of flamboyant, white, befringed Hollywood cowboy costumes. They sang equally synthetic songs like "When the Bloom Is on the Sage."

There were even Indian serenades. My father had two Arapaho friends, chiefs really and truly called White Horse and Black Horse. These imposing gentlemen and their squaws could drive over from the Wind Rivers by way of dangerous Togwotee Pass. They would deliver orations about brotherhood, after a drink or two, and would occasionally beat drums and chant.

July 3, 1930: Blackhorse and Whitehorse came about eight o'clock to drum. They had some supper and afterward went over to the dance cabin. We sat around the fire, and they sang and beat on a tom-tom; some of the songs were particularly strange and beautiful (Blackhorse's Sun Dance songs). There was and is a brilliant half-moon. The air is thin and clear and electric. The stars seem wonderfully alive. Got some firecrackers at Jackson for tomorrow.

One year our Arapaho visitors made rain. This was a serious and effective enterprise; the rain came down, and as a result they had a terrible time getting back over slippery Togwotee Pass. The following year, when asked to break the drought once more by making rain again, they were understandably dubious. They refused at first; but there was a second-hand Ford on the ranch that they wanted, and they finally agreed to make rain if a certain low price could be arranged. They made rain. It poured. They probably drove that very same

Ford back across to the reservation. One or both of the chiefs were deacons of the Episcopalian mission at Ethete.

As a special treat, a gesture of kindness to my parents, when I was little, the Indians made a wickiup outside my cabin windows by weaving together the tops of willows. In this bower they sat crosslegged and drummed me to sleep. The sound of the river, the diminishing drumbeats (much as I wanted to stay awake to hear them) were only too effective. Not many of us have been drummed to sleep by Indian chiefs named Black Horse and White Horse.

3.

ROUGHNECKS AND TENDERFEET

NOBODY seems to use the terms "roughneck" and "tenderfoot" any more. Back when I was a small child I remember reading an early production of my mother's titled "Tommy Tenderfoot." It appeared in an English children's magazine called *Little Folk*. My father, in the *Diary of a Dude Wrangler* written in 1922, still used both terms freely. Sixty years seem to have made them obsolete. They are less specific than "dude" and "outfit" and far more indigenous than "native" and "tourist."

A tenderfoot was obviously any greenhorn in the West, whether a dude or not, someone of civilized delicacy and stupidity who didn't know, quite literally, the ropes and was not broken to hard usage. The roughneck was his experienced opposite. Some dudes were tenderfeet, some not; the outfit was composed of roughnecks almost as a matter of course; but dudes and outfit were such by virtue of economics. The dude paid, the outfit was paid, and expertise in the hills had nothing to do with it. The world's greatest guide or bronc twister was a dude if he was a paying guest on a dude ranch, the milkiest collegian was part of the outfit if he was employed there. So it's too bad, in the interests of both accuracy and picturesqueness, that the old terms have faded away.

A lot of effort was made by old-line dude wranglers like my

father to convince their dudes that there was nothing pejorative about their title. This, however, was not and is not true. When the term was first used out West, at the end of the nineteenth century, it was a common slang term all over the nation for any fancy-pants young man who wore a boutonniere and parted his hair in the middle. There was something dreadfully effete and class-conscious about parting your hair in the middle. Before he went to the Dakotas, Theodore Roosevelt was always described by newspapers as a dude who parted his hair in the middle. The term thus began as derogatory. The only thing that has made it less derogatory is the presence of huge numbers of tourists, "tourist" being even more derogatory. Real dudes, old habitual regular year-after-year roughneck dudes, have become proud of their designation, particularly in relation to tourists. Real dude ranches do and should call themselves that and not the nasty-nice "guest ranch" that appears usually as a designation for overnight places that are really off-the-road tourist camps. It's like "mortician" for undertaker and "hose" for stockings. As for "tourist" and "dude," they are entirely different breeds.

Our ranch, the Bar BC, was of course, as a dude ranch, divided into three general social groups: the dudes, who supported the enterprise; the outfit, who took care of them; and the small enclave of partner-owners, who ran both. As a miniature member of the third group, I naturally considered myself a roughneck. Much as I might like dudes personally, I always preferred to identify myself with the outfit. My proudest and happiest, if most nervous, moments were any spent tagging along with wranglers, bringing the horses down from the flats at dawn, sending them up the benches in the evening. This would entail eating that rich, heavy, early breakfast. I tried to learn how to milk the cows, and did help catch horses and saddle them up for the day's riding. I soulfully watched horse-shoes being made to fit in the heat of the blacksmith's furnace and the tedious yet sometimes rather dramatic process of shoe-ing, the shoer in a blackened leather apron holding the hind foot of the horse between his knees, facing outward in case the horse kicked. Some horses hated shoeing, so they would have to be tied down with a pole between their trussed legs, resulting in much grunting and groaning, eyes rolling with ter-ror and fury.

Then there was horse branding, in theory a brutal operation; but as a rule the blindfolded horse hardly felt the light flick of the red-hot iron on his flank, and the scabby wound healed quickly. The business of cattle branding was more bloodthirsty —calves roped and thrown ("throwed" is Western correct) squalling in the dust, their flailing legs tied together (hogtied), and the not-so-polite business of castration—what in fact made calves into steers.

We had annual roundups at Cow Lake, a flat pond north of the pothole country. My father ran cattle from a ranch down on the Grovont River, the Lower Bar BC; the cattle ranged on the flats north of us. I, unfortunately, never knew very much about this cattle business. I suppose that if I had really wanted enough to be a true roughneck, a part of the outfit, I would have somehow surrendered myself to an initiation. It has al-ways been a load of guilt and a reproach by myself to myself that in fact I never really wanted to, and never really forced myself to learn all the things I ought to have learned. I have often wondered exactly why, given all the opportunities, I was so laggard and missed so many occasions. My father certainly encouraged me, without ever bullying me. He could do all these things himself, some of them well, and would have been an ideal teacher. I was never consciously rebellious, and always admired my father and his abilities. He, in turn, never tried to force me; perhaps he should have. I never had any excuses for dislike and aversion, and in fact it was not aversion but timidity and laziness that held me back. There was talk of me going one summer down to the Lower Ranch to learn something about cattle, but unfortunately nothing came of it. I was too happy on the Upper Ranch.

The sad fact of the matter was that, despite all my western snobbery and feelings of identification, I was by nature and temperament more of a dude, if not exactly a tenderfoot, than I was a roughneck. What interested me, from my beginnings, was never the mechanics, prowess, and achievements of ranching, but the beauties, natural curiosities, and poetry of my native country—with the result, I suppose, that eventually I became a writer instead of a rancher. But it's too bad. My father was both a real ranchman and a real writer; and so I suppose, as his psychologist-partner Horace Carncross could have told us if we'd thought of asking, I managed to work it so that, try as I would (and I did try), I couldn't seem to learn things like roping and fishing. I also turned resolutely away from any thought of becoming a professional writer.

My world then was divided between these two areas—the envied, admired, but for me always just inaccessible world of the Outfit and Roughneck, and the despised but always more familiar and congenial world of the Dude and Tenderfoot. Bill Jump, Jim Budge, Fred Deyo, Cal Carrington—these are a few of the characteristic names I carry in my memory, surrounded by the aura of glamour and expertise associated with wranglers and guides, ropers and horse breakers, as I grew up around them. But I remember little specifically about most of them as people. I knew how they treated horses with a mixture of

53

affection, callousness, care, amusement, irritation—the low, steady drone of curses that so shocked some dudes and delighted others; the grave deliberation in all movements derived from dealing with spooky animals; the quiet, quick sureness in each act of horse catching, saddling, mounting—precision, economy, grace, effectiveness.

All these Westerners always wore "native costume" as a matter of course. This made one of the great distinctions between the outfit and the dudes. On Westerners that costume looked the way it was meant to look, the way it never quite looked on any dudes, ever. The basic work costume was that then despised and plebian getup, the blue work shirt and blue denim Levis ("overalls," never jeans). Other essentials of the costume were the big hat and, around the corral, boots. Hats were worn at all times except in sleep. It was and is and always will be a costume that is practical, protective, and, almost accidentally, becoming. It is also durable and, except for hats and boots, cheap. The blue shirt and blue overalls and heavy wool socks and long-legged union suit were available anywhere at any crossroads store, in any mail-order catalog. Another important and cheap adjunct to the costume then was the neckerchief, worn loose around the neck—usually, like the most common handkerchief, a colorful red or blue bandana.

Overalls were strictly for work, and a true Westerner did not wear them to a dance. I remember, not so very long ago, the shock and disgust of well-dressed Westerners when dude kids appeared at a dressed-up square dance in dirty blue jeans, thinking of course that they were being terribly "native." This was before the Levi had conquered the whole world of youth. The cowboy Saturday-night dress shirt was a sight to be seen, no holds barred, harlequin colors, embroidered butterflies, silver buttons, God knows what. For funerals and perhaps other lugubrious occasions, one might wear store clothes (with big hats and boots, of course), and all the men would look pretty awkward. But the memory of a dear departed, especially female, demanded this sacrifice of dignity and looks. Hats were then removed, too.

Unfortunately this "Western" or "cowboy" costume is not one that is easy to wear properly, and on anyone but the lean-hipped prototype it tends to look awful. Nothing shows up a middle-aged pot or a fanny more mercilessly, even shorts. Any kind of flabbiness and flimsiness leaps to the eye, especially the eye of the Westerner looking at an Easterner trying to look like a Westerner. Starchy, ill-fitting Levis belted up around a bulging waist and exposing ankles and store shoes, the big hat plopped awkwardly on top of the unaccustomed head, the loose or nervous gestures and sloppy gait betraying ignorance of horses—this only too common middle-aged caricature is an integral part of the Western disdain for everybody else.

In the old days, before 1930, nobody wore Western costume except Westerners, with the exception of pseudo-Western Hollywood actors; and their costumes were fantastic white travesties of any real thing. One of the big changes of going from East to West was this change of costume. Nobody wore Levis in the East. If you saw, as you sometimes did, an Ivy League college boy in what has come to be mislabeled "blue jeans," you could be sure he had been out on a ranch during the summer. So the division between East and West began right with clothes and how you looked in them. The sign of acclimatization of a dude was frequently the degree to which he adapted himself to Western costume and looked at home in it; but even the most seasoned dude tended to look a bit different somehow—a bit less taut, a little less swagger.

Another chasm between dude and outfit was speech. Into that chasm we half-breeds fell with a thud. As much as learning to roll our own cigarettes, or playing a dead-pan game of poker, learning to curse out a horse with natural fluency was a goal, a grail. But unfortunate exposure to a back-East education and the influence of family and the dude children we played with during the summer cured us of any legitimate "western accent," including the curious obligatory grammatical dialect a real Westerner would always tend to use. It was impossible to master locutions like "them sonsabitches took and lit out" or "where them horses was at" without being self-conscious. Garl German's (pronounced "Gurman") dictum on Poe's "Raven" — that "it don't make any damn sense, but it sure is *wrote*" is the proper Western way to express it; but even as an adolescent I couldn't swing it. To this day I can't even properly imitate a "Western accent."

That there should be such a thing as a Western accent at all is in defiance of every conceivable sort of modern cant. For a good hundred years or more everyone who writes has been going on about the steady standardization of life by books, newspapers, education, mobility, the theater, the movies, the radio, and now, of course, television. Creeping civilization. Yet during just exactly that period, and only then — not conceivably before those hundred years — a distinct regional accent has been created and still flourishes. It must derive from an older Appalachian brogue imported across Kentucky and Missouri and up from Texas and Oklahoma, shedding some of its southern drawls and picking up some twangy Middle Westernisms — what used to be called "Pike County." It still has lots of drawl and twang but seems to be characterized mainly by an odd sort of emphasis on usually unstressed syllables (DU-bois, for instance) and, of course, by its peculiar grammar and vocabulary. "Ornery critters" really is a native locution and "them horses was" always correct for "those horses were."

One sure way, then, that you could tell a dude was by his accent. Since many early dudes, as opposed to tourists, were Eastern upper class, the gap was wide. Accents that would have sounded outlandish to natives of Kansas City or Spokane sounded even more peculiar in Jackson Hole. People like the Countess who spoke with an intercontinental husky drawl, with a sting at the end, or Mrs. de Rham who had the most fluty, Newporty broad-**A** accent—she always referred to her "r-r-ahnsh"—set a standard of dude talk that could hardly be exceeded in exoticism by Chinese mandarins. About all that dudes and roughnecks shared in this line was a theoretical use of the so-called English language, and also that they didn't speak with all-Amurican [sic] Middle-Western accents.

One thing that dudes and roughnecks always did have in common was love of the country. Some dudes never got used to it, but others were as noxiously enthusiastic as recent Catholic converts. Nobody was a more famous and vocal convert than the famous Countess, née in Chicago as Eleanor Patterson but always called Cissy, heir of Joseph Medill, kin of the McCormicks, married with glamorous misfortune to an egregious Pole, Count Gisycki.

After a hair-raising escape from her brutal husband's decaying estate in deepest Poland, in the depths of winter, clutching her daughter Felicia to her bosom and no doubt pursued by wolves, she ended up somewhat later on the Bar BC in a state of emotional collapse with seven trunks and a French maid. This dramatic entrance, as of 1916, is chronicled in the *Diary of a Dude Wrangler*. One of the annual Bar BC Fancy Dress Parties was in full swing and my mother had to greet the travel-worn but fearsomely chic Countess as a "cave woman" dressed in furs.

The French maid wept for twenty-four hours and was sent off. The Countess complained about everything, and no day passed without a fight with my father. They both enjoyed this, being of generally Irish extraction; besides, the Countess was a notoriously provocative woman, red-haired, cat-faced, tiger-tempered, full of vim and viperishness. Like many another supersophisticate, she fell for the West, especially its more primitive aspects. Not only the flora but the fauna. Cal Carrington, a lank, sardonic, prune-faced guide, profane and dictatorial (he appears as "Nate" in the *Diary*) was rather reluctantly swept into her flaming orbit.

They first got entangled during a memorable hunting trip up Soda Fork. There were just the three of them: Cal, the Countess, and young Felicia. During snowy days in the tent Cissy read aloud from *War and Peace*. As a final result, Cissy took Cal away from the Bar BC, much to my father's annoyance, and set him up as her own foreman on her own ranch, up in the Grovonts, on Flat Creek. She took him East to Washington, sent him on safaris in Africa and tours of the Continent, and in general conducted with him what certainly appeared to be one of the Hole's more flamboyant dude-cowboy affairs. Anyone else might have been spoiled, but Cal was a match for the iron whim of the lady and was in his own way just as ornery and self-protective. This love-battle has been variously described in three biographies of Eleanor Patterson, but the best and eyewitness account is that in Felicia's articles for *Vogue* (of all places) and the local *Teton Magazine*.[1]

---

[1] Felicia Gisycka Magruder, "Cissy Patterson, the Countess of Flat Creek," *Teton Magazine* 10 (1977). Of the three book-length biographies, the latest, *Cissie*, by Ralph G. Martin (Simon and Schuster, 1979), is full of egregious little errors about her Western

Cissy went on to become a spectacular figure in the family tradition of newspapering. As owner-editor of the *Washington Herald* she quarreled with the city of Washington and the various presidents and their wives. The long friendship-feud with Alice Roosevelt Longworth, spiked with juicy incidents, made social history in a capital full of such feuds. The two women were too much alike to coexist peacefully in the same circles. Her Western friends were royally entertained in her mansion on Dupont Circle or the later Dower House. My father resumed his arguments with her there, spread over increasingly longer intervals. He, as a rabid New Dealer and anti-Hitler interventionist, found her attitudes harder and harder to take, especially her isolationism.

Rose Crabtree, the smart-as-a-whip owner and manager of the Crabtree Hotel in Jackson (where we had that room with the grand piano in it on rodeo night), and Cal Carrington continued their friendships; but the Countess came to her ranch less and less as the years went on and finally not at all. Only her daughter Felicia and her cousins, the Albrights further east in Wyoming, kept up active Western connections in modern times.

Frances Mears could not have presented an example of a dude-cowboy romance with more contrast. She came out from Philadelphia to the Bar BC in charge of her handsome but psychopathic brother Bryant. Dad was supposed to reform him. Bryant spent a couple of years in the Hole threatening and even attempting to shoot my father, happily without success. Frances fell in love with the sturdiest and solidest of cowboys, Buster Estes. They settled down to marriage and ranching and lived happily ever afterwards—very different

experiences—names spelled wrong (like Irvin Course for Irving Corse), "Cissie" shooting mountain goat in the Grovonts instead of sheep, etc.

from the more glamorous but less stable fling of Cal and the Countess.

The Hunt-Scott saga repeated in later days some of the atmospherics of the Gisycka-Carrington collision. In 1927, at a place called the Elbo Ranch, there appeared an elegant woman called Madame Gibaud. Of all the encroachments of modernism into our part of the country in the late twenties—the Jenny Lake dance hall, various nasty little roadside tourist camps and hot dog stands—the Elbo was the most conspicuous and offensive. It was situated up on Cottonwood, just where our Bar BC road turned off, and though calling itself a dude, or no doubt "guest," ranch, it was more properly a tourist camp, taking travelers in off the graveled highway. It advertised itself with a huge billboard proclaiming the "Elbo Ranch, Home of Hollywood Cowboys," and was run by a California entrepreneur called Goss.

Madame Gibaud arrived there fresh from Paris and the celebration over Lindbergh's crossing. She had shed one M. Gibaud, a no-account Parisian, in the process. She shortly took back the name of her first husband, a more amiable New Yorker called Hunt, and was ever afterwards called Elena Hunt. She liked the country, if not necessarily the Elbo and Mr. Goss, and there met that suave cowboy-of-the-world Gib Scott, then the Elbo foreman. Gib was a knowledgeable and successful horse and lady handler, and soon Elena and Gib became partners on their own ranch in the south of the valley, becoming a valley institution on the same stylish plane as Cissy and Cal.

Elena was a small, dark, hawk-nosed, bright-eyed, nervous woman with a hoarse, commanding voice, who looked as though any high wind might blow her away, but who was a dynamo of grit and energy. She raised and broke her own horses, preferably for races in which she herself rode. She made a horse-racing bet with a local aviator, as a result of which she learned to solo an airplane after the age of seventy; all this despite the fact that as she grew older she was hampered by a progressively severe vertigo, and often was too dizzy to stay on her horse. That never stopped her from riding. Despite her frail health and family disasters, Elena remained indomitable, caustic, and high-spirited, one of the Hole's best-known and best-loved characters till her death in 1965.

One of the most remarkable mementos of Jackson Hole history is a tape made by Josephine Fabian as part of her invaluable oral history project: Elena describing her own life in her own rather hoarse voice and very frank words—her background as daughter of an adventurous mining tycoon, her earlier marriage and life in New York and Paris, and finally the tales of her arrival in the Hole and subsequent adventures. It is a classic.

Jeanne de Rham, who along with Cissy and Elena carried on this peculiar local tradition of stock-raising grandes dames, differed in being far more conventional. Though sufficiently intrepid as a ranchwoman and raiser of prize bulls, she did not have the same picturesque liaisons. She had been one of three elegant daughters of a socially ambitious Newport contractor. One daughter married a French baron, one married a Philadelphia millionaire, and Jeanne married a member of a distinguished French-American family of New York. Charles de Rham, her husband, was killed in World War I. The most famous member of that family in this century was a Willie de Rham who ran a select dancing class in New York without losing caste.[2]

<hr />

[2]I believe it still exists. As for Jeanne and her bulls, she once exhibited a prize bull at a local fair. A man with fourteen children very much wanted to see this bull, but

Jeanne first came to the JY, then bought her own place up against the Grovonts northeast of Jackson. There her relations descended on her. Most notorious of these were her French connections, children of the baroness sister. There was a nice, priggish, earnest young baron, and there was his affected but nonetheless sexy sister, married, like Cissy, to a Polish nobleman. This little group cut quite a swathe, especially since the prince carried on the Continental tradition exemplified by Count Gisycki of insolvency and seduction. His main object, it was generally assumed in the valley where secrets are open, was to get hold of the de Rham r-r-ahnsh for himself. He came close to succeeding. Jeanne evidently planned to have him manage it for her; but something went wrong and in his pique he made unflattering remarks about Mrs. de Rham to his brother-in-law, the baron, at a picnic down by the Snake River. The Baron slapped him in the face with his glove and challenged him to a duel. What might have been Jackson Hole's first formal affair of honor, as opposed to plain old-fashioned shoot-out, was frustrated by the fact that both partners chose the same man as their second. He was able to dissuade the baron and so prevented this historic occasion from actually taking place. The prince and princess left shortly afterwards. Jeanne de Rham died in the same year as Elena, 1965, and her ranch was sold.

After Elena there seems to be no successor to this fifty-year-old tradition of high-toned East-West romance. Another couple, a rather reclusive artist called Paul Coburn and his lady friend, handsome Mrs. Wilson, lived on the beautiful Aspen Ranch down below the JY. Rosemary Wilson, Mrs. Wilson's daughter, was the belle of the valley among the younger dude-

___

could not afford admission for the family. "Come in, come in free," Jeanne is supposed to have said. "I want my bull to see *you*."

ranching set back there in the midthirties. The Coburn-Wilson ménage was a rather staid one, like that of Miss Noble and Sidney, and they were also both Easterners, but certainly not married ones.

One evening after a rodeo during the thirties Jeanne de Rham gave a little party at the Bluebird Cafe, of which I was, I guess, the only other unattached member. The other guests included Elena and Gib and Paul Coburn and Mrs. Wilson. Champagne was served, wrapped in a napkin by the rather nervous waitress, a local girl whom everyone knew, and it was pretty festive. At one point, however, Mrs. de Rham was inspired to say coyly, apropos of God knows what, "All the bachelors at the table raise their hands!" A more sheepish pair of hands raised than those of Gib Scott and Paul Coburn has never been seen.

Another clutch of local nobility is German and still holds forth down country. These are the von Gontards, connections of Anheuser-Busch, and their further noble connections, the Seher Thosses. Everybody is baroness or count and aside from a slight pall during the war, when it was suspected that they were not perhaps a hundred percent anti-German, they have mostly managed to stay on the bright side of publicity. There was some Seher-Thoss bar brawling at one time, but the chief representative of the clan for many years, Baroness Consuela von Gontard, was one of the best-hearted queens of the valley, devoted to culture and, in true German tradition, founder and backer of the local summer festival symphony orchestra. She was apt to appear to her guests on her Melody Ranch down country dressed as for a garden party in wide hat and droopy skirts and not exactly sure where the party was actually being held, at the moment. This lovable representative of grande-damerie, surrounded by handsome, hard-riding, polo-playing children, was the last of these queens of the valley to go, dying in 1969. With her passing this particular aspect of Jackson Hole life seems to be extinguished.

Although I knew all these ladies and mingled to a varying extent with their younger kin, they were contemporaries of my parents, and not much part of my own personal experience. My closest dude friends were naturally children of my own age, with whom I tried to play the roughneck, summer after summer, and generally introduce them, with superior aplomb, into the mysteries of Our Country. I must have been pretty insufferable. Peter Borie, son of Adolph the painter who was the Bar BC's first dude, was a rebellious playmate. My parents remembered one incident of his slavery. My sister and he were playing house, she cooking, he in bed. Peter was heard to whimper plaintively, "Can't I get up now?" "No," said my sister firmly. "You're the gentleman and I'm the cook and you can't get up till breakfast is ready." Since Peter was a testy, didactic, and stubborn redhead, we had a generally stormy time trying to control him. There was a Boston girl called Mary Warren, who, since she was bigger and even bossier than we were, had us under *her* thumb.

Oldest and best and most continuous of our playmates were the Galeys. We had been given a pair of donkeys, and spent many painful moments trying to ride them. Being definitely roughnecks themselves, not dudes, the donkeys had us where they wanted us. Sometimes they would let us get on them, but after a while they would deliberately brush us off on a low aspen branch or scrape us against a fence post, or simply hump up in the middle. No objections or pleas on our part made any difference.

One summer day, when I was about five, I was told to go

greet and entertain a family of just-arrived Philadelphia dudes, the widowed Mrs. Frank Galey (Marion) and her four children (Eleanor, Marion, Helen, and Frank, Jr.). I reluctantly went over, dragging my equally reluctant donkey. As a gesture of hospitality I placed the oldest girl, Eleanor, on one end of the donkey and put myself on the other. The donkey waited till we were safely settled, then humped. As we went off in different directions a friendship was established that, unique among those made as children on the Bar BC, has lasted to this day. The Galeys came again and again, we saw them often in the East and even spent a winter sharing a villa on the Riviera together. All through childhood we were Best Friends.

Their later history was connected not with the Bar BC but the White Grass. The White Grass was the third dude ranch in the Hole. As the Bar BC was an offshoot of the JY, when my father finally couldn't stand Joy any longer and split off, taking a share of JY dudes, so the White Grass was a more amicable offshoot of the Bar BC. It was started around 1913 by a most unlikely combination of East and West, Harold Hammond and Tucker Bispham. Harold was a sober but genial wrangler at the Bar BC, anything but the "romantic cowboy," but a good hand. Tucker was of course the orchidaceous Max Beerbohm of Princeton '04, who courted my Aunt Polly with Swinburnian poetry and was followed about Oxford by his valet, Nurser.

It is rather hard to know just what inspired Tucker to go into dude ranching. Perhaps disappointment in love. My aunt was captured from him by an even more flamboyantly fin-de-siècle character, a pseudoliterary figure named Reginald Roberts. He arrived on the ranch fresh from a semitriumphant career in London where, as a startlingly handsome and at that time startlingly rich product of all that was exotic and luxurious of Santa Barbara in 1900, he turned into one of those lions that London used to like. He had "literary ambitions," published a slim volume of poems, knew all sorts of people famous at that time, and in general was able to over-trump Tucker Bispham in every direction. Tucker was far from handsome, being short and monkey faced and moustached. Tucker had not published a slim volume. Tucker had not gone on Santa Barbara picnics with silk tents and silverware. Tucker's family was embedded in Philadelphia law, respectable but not very romantic. Reggie's stepfather was the dashing poet Cameron Rogers who had written the words of "The Rosary" as a love poem to Reggie's mother. ("Each hour a pearl, each pearl a prayer . . . O memories that bless and burn.") The very brunette Reggie had been nicknamed the "Black Pearl" in consequence.

Polly had a special little cabin built for her among the aspens on the Bar BC made not of logs like all the other cabins but of pine slabs, with a high one-way slanting roof and window shutters prettily painted by Polly herself, she being a talented if lazy artist. It definitely had the look of a Studio. There Tucker and Reggie spent their days either fiercely grubbing sagebrush from around the outside or having long soulful conversations with Polly on the inside, mixed with poetry and muttered curses at each other. Reggie won. Polly and Reggie left the ranch to go on to their honeymoon and soon discovered that one of Reggie's uncles had mismanaged his affairs and he was penniless.

He felt himself totally incapacitated for life in this cruel world and spent the rest of his existence, ably abetted by Polly, living off other people, notably his mother and my hardworking parents, whom he despised as literary hacks. He never even wrote poetry, devoting himself largely to making excerpts from the English poets, which he copied into numberless notebooks. These quotations dealt with such things as insomnia, dyspepsia, melancholia, and illness—a sort of Rosary of Gloom. John Keats, Samuel Taylor Coleridge, William Wordsworth, and Percy Bysshe Shelley all in their own words demonstrated that the life of a poet was not a happy one, just like Reggie's; but all through my childhood and adolescence the Roberts remained my ideals of charm and sophistication.

So Tucker in his disappointment became a partner of Harold Hammond on the White Grass, siphoning off part of the Bar BC's stream of Philadelphia dudes. Their brand was H⌣B (Hammond quarter circle Bispham). Harold married an engaging, hardworking wife named Marie, and between them they built up and ran the White Grass. It has a pretty situation, nestled against the Tetons in a big meadow covered with the little plant called "whitegrass" that gave the ranch its name. Smaller than either the JY or the Bar BC, the White Grass had a more homogeneous and intimate atmosphere with a heavy Philadelphia accent. Among the dudes siphoned off from the Bar BC were the Galeys. Tucker spent his summers there reading from his extensively erudite library, each book marked with his crested bookplate, and occasionally losing himself in the woods. "I'm a damned dude, always was a damned dude, and always will be a damned dude, and proud of it," he liked to proclaim. Eventually he too married.

In 1921 three spinsters from New York, a doctor, a nurse, and a social worker, came to the White Grass and Tucker married one of them, Helen Sloan (the social worker). When Marie Hammond died, Harold married Marion Galey. The Bisphams retired from active partnership. Harold died, Marion inherited the White Grass from him, and her son Frank Galey,

Jr., in turn inherited it from her. It is the last of the three original ranches still in operation as a true dude ranch. As such it is the oldest in the valley.

Most of the later dude ranches and dude-owned ranches, until the fifties at least, were the offspring of these originals. The Huylers for instance, who once made candy and lived in Greenwich, were dudes at the Circle H. The depression did unfortunate things to candy, and when it started to melt away, Coulter Huyler decided dude ranching was a safer bet. He started operations at his ranch, the Bear Paw, also up against the Tetons in a line with the JY and the White Grass, and for years it was one of the best in the valley. It was distinguished by the fact that southern Mrs. Huyler did not approve of liquor —very unlike the Bar BC, especially in its later phases. An exotic teetotaling atmosphere prevailed. Teetotaling is about as characteristic of Wyoming as white-tie and tails. This did not seem to inhibit the popularity of the Bear Paw, however. Eventually Coulter Huyler retired to his own private spread, the Rocking H, now owned by his son Jack.

Many other dude ranches followed the White Grass, some by now old and well-established places with their own fanatical following like the Triangle X and the Trail Creek. Ranches originally bought by Bar BC dudes for their own use, like the Frew's 4 Lazy F or the Dilworth's Circle H, later on turned into dude ranches. In nearly every case there is some connection between the later and the earlier ranches—a Western partner that worked on one of the older places, an Eastern partner who had been there as a dude. Though the two originals, the Bar BC and the JY, no longer operate as true dude ranches, their descendants, whether as private ranches or as active dude ranches, still proliferate.

One of the more startling of Bar BC descendants was the Woodward camp on Leigh Lake facetiously named Bar None (that is, universal hospitality). Dr. Woodward and his large family had been early dudes at the Bar BC. Mrs. Woodward, a Pennsylvania railroad heiress, was a small, calm, determined woman, famous for her lavish hospitality in her mansion in Chestnut Hill, near Philadelphia, where stately musicales were given. At one of these, while receiving, her underpants fell down and she handed them to the butler without interrupting her hospitality or changing expression.

Dr. Woodward was tall, lanky, and professorial. He was a sure-enough medical doctor, but never practiced. He gave himself up to learned hobbies. He found the Bar BC too luxurious and moved up to the Bar None so he could live in jolly discomfort, the simple life with a vengeance. My father, who always believed in being as comfortable as circumstances permitted, looked askance on all this, as did most Westerners. The Doctor's eccentricities added to the local sarcasm. He always wore pepper-and-salt plus fours and a little canvas boating hat, as though he were on Mount Desert. One day he was expostulating to a group of Bar BC wranglers on the virtues of this hat—excellent for drinking water out of, could be folded in the pocket. "Good for everything except a hat," was the Western comment. He believed firmly in higher things, and on rides would sit on his horse backward, legs folded over the cantle of his saddle, reading Shakespeare aloud to his family as they followed along behind him—no mean feat.

Almost as great a contrast as contrasts could be to the Spartanism of the Bar None was the Frew's 4 Lazy F. This beautiful outfit, also given a facetious name (the four lazy Frews being Mr., Mrs., and the two girls, Emily and Peggy), came into being in 1926 just above the Ferry and just below Cottonwood

Creek and the Bar BC. It was intended as a fishing ranch, with its own reach of the Snake River at the back door and out the front a lushly irrigated lawn among cottonwoods. The main cabin was and is one of the most tastefully magnificent interiors in the Hole, filled with antiques from older houses in Pittsburgh and handmade Western furniture. More recent additions have been the pictures, some of the best of them painted by Henry Oliver, the Frew's son-in-law.

Equally vivid as personalities, of course, and sometimes equally eccentric, were the members of the outfit, those "roughnecks" we children admired so wholeheartedly and uncritically. There is hardly a Jackson Hole family of pioneer vintage that didn't at some time and in some capacity have some member of it working at the Bar BC ranches, upper or lower. Of the long list a few stand out in my memory as special heroes.

The most notable was our foreman, Joe LePage. With only one good eye and a rather raffish black patch on the other, French-Canadian with a fairly strong accent, Joe combined a traditional loyalty to the outfit with a deep personal friendship with my father. Feudal loyalty to the particular outfit one works for is commonplace in the West, but it is not invariably coupled with admiration for the owner. Joe ran the working side of the ranch, particularly the horses, and it was he who taught us to ride and permitted us to tag along while he did things. He could have taught me to do those things—cow milking, horseshoeing—if I had let him. Of all my father's Western friends, he was the closest, and appeared most often in my father's writings, either as himself in the *Diary* or as a fictional character in *The Delectable Mountains*.

Like Carncross, he was single, but not necessarily a bachelor. There were rumors of a wife back up in Canada somewhere.

Late in life he married for sure a round-faced, bouncy California schoolteacher who tried to elevate his tastes and decorate his cabin. I remember her painting an elk-hide screen with a mountain view. Puffy little clouds filled the top of the composition, and I never see such puffy little clouds in real life without thinking of Dorothy LePage's elk-hide screen. They moved up the river later on to a ranch and cabin of their own, and had a son. We used to ride up and visit them and drink lemonade and listen to Sears Roebuck records of "Shoo Fly, Don't Bother Me." She more or less deserted him, or at least went off to California in the winter with her son and left him in his lonely cabin to die during a blizzard, too far from help.

The other two members of the outfit who dominated our childhood were the two pack-trip guides, George Ross and Frank Giles. They presented a Mutt and Jeff contrast. George was a tall, slim, very handsome fellow with dark hair, a hooked nose, and a sort of Indian Chief look of dignity and reserve. Frank was a small, rather weasel-faced fellow, quiet spoken and ironic. They were furiously jealous of each other, but both ferociously outfit-proud. They were both men of extensive families, with many children, some still in the valley, and represented the stable, ranch-owning pioneer settler sort of Westerner, as opposed to the dude-girl susceptible wranglers, or wild men like Cal Carrington.

These latter added spice to the setup, especially for the dude girls, but were definitely not "stable." They came and they went. Joe and George and Frank stayed. Equally transitory and decorative were the cabin girls, "cabin girl" being a generic term that covered waitresses, laundresses, and girls who actually made up the dudes' cabins. I have a romanticized picture of them, derived probably from adolescent years — a series

71

of blooming local peaches. There were gorgeous blondes like Lillian, who became Mrs. Jess Wort, or the starry-eyed goddess from Idaho who spelled her name ORa, capital O, capital R, little a. Tucker Bispham's nursery rhyme sums up this impression of a bevy (dictionary: a collection of roes, quails, or larks) of beauties and their often exotic names:

> Twila Lila Lou,
> Twila Lila Lee,
> Twila Lila Lillian Vivian,
> That's the girl for me.

I was too young to be of any interest to any of them. Many snatched the wranglers away from the dude girls; after all, the dudes went home after Labor Day and the cabin girls frequently did not. There were many such wrangler–cabin-girl matches, but I can't think of any male–dude–cabin-girl ones. Not enough eligible male dudes perhaps. There were plenty of dude-dudene marriages though.

All of these married couples are grandparents by now, or could be, East or West. No doubt the memory of those long summer twilights with the banjos or the guitars twanging and young people cavorting or making love round about the dance cabin provides a fund of nostalgia and is an integral part of the "Old West" of an aging generation. For my parents it provided a good deal in the way of headaches. For me it was all part of the mysteriousness of grown-up life.

Of all the Bar BC wranglers, I remember best those from a later time, the end of the twenties before we moved up to the Three Rivers, or the early thirties when we still rode down to the Bar BC from Pacific Creek: people like Walt Callahan, the pint-sized rodeo king, who could outride everyone twice his size, or long-nosed Bill Tanner, wry and humorous. The most spectacular roughnecks of this later period were the Emerys. There was Hugh, who liked to have his name pronounced "Ug"—a big, kindly fellow already mentioned as a source of songs—and his not at all kindly brother John. John was a legend in his time, and one of the few would-be murderers we really knew personally. He was a big, strong, dark, handsome man, with a definitely Indian cast of countenance. It was pretty obvious that he was not to be trifled with.

One of the institutions that typified the increasingly raffish Hole at the end of the twenties and on for the next decade was the dance halls. There were two in particular that I knew, one on Jenny Lake and one right outside of Jackson on the road north. They were rather good-looking log buildings with polished floors and discreet decor, and every Saturday night in summer they were centers of gaiety and mayhem. People stomped about in boots to the music of Glen Exum, then a college student, later a famous mountain climber. This was the gaiety. The mayhem usually went on offstage, either automobile accidents as the drunken drivers wove away from the scene of the gaiety, or the inevitable fights that took place as the evening wore on and the tempers wore thin. One of the principal causes of mayhem was John Emery. John when drunk liked to fight. Brother Hugh when drunk liked to watch John fight. Nearly every weekend Ug would egg some patron of some dance hall on to injure John's feelings. They were easily injured; whereupon John would beat the customer to a pulp, much to Hugh's satisfaction. The fact that another brother, Olin Emery, was a sometime sheriff added spice to these family affairs.

One of John's more picturesque exploits, which he liked to tell of around a campfire, was the time he bit off an acquaintance's nose. John was playing poker in Jackson and the acquaintance, whom John didn't like much anyway, was kibitzing over his shoulder. He kept needling John and finally, in an excess of folly, rubbed his nose against the back of John's neck. It was, according to John, a big dirty nose. John turned around and bit it off. That fixed the kibitzer.

More dramatic and romantic was the legend of John's attempt to shoot and kill a rival in love. John and Fred Holmson were courting beautiful Dollie Rose, and Fred seemed to be winning. John, in the heat of passion, came up behind Fred while he was shaving and shot him. It looked as though John had gone too far this time. He was arrested and put in jail, the first incumbent of the new but still unfinished structure. It was a sturdy building except for the roof, which was made temporarily of plywood. John seemed somehow to have possession of a hunting knife. He cut a hole through the ceiling and escaped. This was in the dead of winter, but John, on foot, made his way through a five-foot snow some sixty miles to Dubois, and hence out of the jurisdiction of the county sheriff. Togwotee Pass, around 9,500 feet high, was completely blocked in those days with winter snowdrifts. Teton county couldn't get him back; and in any case Fred recovered, forgave John, saying that he would have done the same in his place, and married Dollie.

When they were married, John came back to the valley, but his presence made the newlyweds so nervous that they asked him to leave; and he did. He ended up somewhere in Montana, where supposedly he came to no good end as a, by this time, successful murderer. He was always kind to us younger fry, in a somewhat somber way, and we hung on every one of his lurid words. Others, especially his dance-hall victims and his brother Olin, took a less rosy view of John.

74

Not all our roughneck friends were as rough as that. Unlike my father, we never actually knew murderers of an older generation like the sinister remittance-man Sargent who used to live up on Jackson Lake and who probably murdered his wife, nor the equally sinister Sewell, benign old rancher and solid citizen who had two homesteaders murdered for him when he felt they were encroaching on his range. We never saw Dismal Dick, the South African gentleman of high birth who settled up in the Buffalo Fork region and who had to be shot when he went crazy and stalked his neighbor, Bill Stilson.

The idea that cowboys shot each other up every weekend in the Old West is a considerable exaggeration. Good hands are a valuable commodity. Perhaps at the end of the long cattle drives of the 1870s in wide-open railhead towns, there was a good deal of unnecessary exuberance, but in more settled ranching towns like the old Jackson, barroom brawls took the form of fists, not bullets. True enough, once in a while someone would be overcome by passion, like John Emery, and take to a gun, but not every Saturday night. Fights were rough enough without that, bloody affairs with knockdowns and even trompings; that is, bootheels in the face. Though people might be marred, they were not killed.

Feuds were something else again. The feuders did not shoot each other as a rule. They just refused to talk or associate for years. Bill and Holiday (so named because he was born on Christmas) Menor, one of whom operated the Ferry, frequently refused to speak to each other for long periods, though they were brothers and lived right across the river from each other. Francis Judge has a fine description of this ornery pair,[3] who enjoyed nothing more than abusing each other to some third party.

[3]National Park Service, *Mountain Men*, 1960.

In my father's case the feuds were largely political, based on battles over conservation and park extension. Though hatred ran high, and was usually very personal, this seemed to have no effect on his relationships with some people. Felix Buchenroth, forest ranger and banker, one of the most bitter opponents of the park from the earliest days, was supposed to be one of these monsters of the Opposition; yet he and my father seemed to keep right on seeing and enjoying each other, and he was always up at the Bar BC or the later Three Rivers full of stories, in his heavy German accent, of incredible exploits all over the West and Mexico.

The attempt to transfer the spirit of Appalachia to Wyoming in a movie such as *Spencer's Mountain* illustrated vividly the differences in customs. In Wyoming feuds were personal rather than family matters. Cousins did not go around shooting cousins ad infinitum; nor did Westerners ever go in for secret stills and dead revenue officers. They have always drunk openly and frequently from bottles. Preachers were never treated with teetotaling awe by starchy women folk. A preacher like Royal Balcom—who baptized my sister and me out in an aspen glade, and who created the by now almost too famous Chapel of the Transfiguration, at Moose, with its plate-glass window enshrining the Grand Teton—was anything but a teetotaling Puritan. The log walls of Saint John's, in Jackson, are supposed to be pockmarked with bullet holes put there by a not-so-successful hell-raising incumbent during one of his sprees.

But religion in the Hole is another story, and one that certainly did not have much to do with my childhood. The largest group of local worshipers are the Church of Jesus Christ of Latter-Day Saints; that is, Mormons; but the best-organized and most-prestigious denomination both in the Hole and in Wyoming has been the Episcopalian. The Episcopalians were the first and most active missionaries to the Wyoming Indians; they established the hospital in Jackson that was originally alongside the church; and for years they were the only other churchgoers besides the Mormons that had much community standing. Now, however, almost every branch of Christianity is represented in Jackson, and during the summer the park is full of mountain-climbing young seminarians who conduct services in the open under the auspices of the Christian Ministry to the National Parks.

The names and faces of innumerable other dudes, roughnecks, preachers, and murderers crowd my memory, in a rather confused state of disassociation. In every case some good story lies buried with each face or name, but as far as I am concerned, most of these stories are lost along with so many other aspects of the past of Jackson Hole.

Joe LePage was succeeded as foreman on the Bar BC by that very different character, Bill Howard. Bill was everything that Joe was not—handsome, dashing, a daring and expert rider, full of charm (especially for the ladies), and basically dishonest and disloyal. Though treacherous enough to my father personally, he did display moments of spectacular devotion to the outfit.

There was a terrible and famous fight at one of the slapdash rodeos put on by that ragged outfit, the Elbo. Their makeshift rodeo ground was right out in the middle of our flats and was considered a first-class eyesore. Bill Howard and Ren Chafin, who was foreman of the Lower Bar BC, were deadly enemies on the basis of a rivalry between the two ranches, though they were both owned by my father. High words passed during the Elbo Rodeo that led to fists and cobblestones, and finally Bill

Howard rode off toward the ranch to get a gun. Wiser heads prevailed and eventually peace between the two outfits was patched up. Despite this extreme loyalty to the brand, Bill nonetheless tried to extract every cent he could from the ranch, and the last days of the Bar BC as a running dude ranch were a general wreckage brought about to a considerable extent by Bill's manipulations.

In the twenties a young ex-aviator of World War I named Irving Corse, from Minneapolis, had come to the ranch as a summer wrangler and stayed to become a junior partner. He was one of the more successful examples of the conversion from dude to roughneck. After Horace Carncross died, he became a full partner, and when my father retired in 1930 he took over sole operation of the ranch. He had married a dude girl, Angela Nalle, from Philadelphia, and a more mismatched couple it would be hard to imagine. Irv was a handsome, active, neurotic guy devoted to playing the role of Real Westerner to the hilt, punctuated by intermittent breakdowns based on his harrowing war experiences as an aviator. During these spells all his hair would fall out. Being a Real Westerner took the form of heavy drinking and lavish poker playing, much of both in the company of Bill Howard, who had a good head for both liquor and cards and usually came out winner. Irv had the idea that a Real Western Ranch should be as rundown and dusty as possible. Angela was a highstrung intellectual who read "transition" and advanced poetry. She found Irv's version of the Real West increasingly harder to take. While my parents were around, the personal charms of both Corses were assets, but left to themselves, Irv's indulgences and Angela's dissatisfactions became liabilities.

Into this unstable situation came another couple, the Pavenstedts. Maud Pavenstedt was a charmer, low voiced and quietly seductive, a writer herself, married first to another writer, Richard Washburn Childs, then a divorcée with two pretty little daughters. She came to the ranch unattached. My father was considerably smitten. She then returned with her new husband Edmund Pavenstedt, a Harvard and New York German whose mixture of sophisticated charm and plump petulance pleased some more than others.

When it came time to divide the assets of the Bar BC upon my father's retirement, the partners couldn't agree on a proper split of the "shares." According to custom, a supposedly disinterested friend of both parties was chosen to mediate. Irv and my father each got 49 percent, the Pavenstedts were given the two remaining shares. Maud was supposed to be a dear friend of our family, as well as a crony of the Corses. Almost immediately friction arose about the management of the ranch and the division of profits. The Pavenstedts used their margin of control to ease my father out of any further hand in the business, and it was another one of the valley's numerous feuds. Under the increasingly erratic management of Irv, the profits of the ranch became negligible in any case. The cabins decayed, most of them beyond repair, and there was a serious fire in 1941.

Angela divorced Irv, whose health and nerves became worse and worse. The Howards took off, involved in their own plan for establishing a ranch of their own at somebody else's expense, which in fact never seemed to be established. The only good thing that happened was that Irv found a charming second wife who would have been a far more well-adjusted dude-wrangling partner in the first place. But by then it was too late. The war killed off such business as the Bar BC still had. Irv became increasingly unstable and finally committed suicide. The ranch itself was a shambles — as ramshackle and rundown a specimen of the Real West as Irv could possibly have desired. A whole series of postwar disasters did nothing to help revive its former glories. It does, however, carry on valiantly under the direction of Margaretta Corse, who rents out such cabins as can be restored to housekeeping summer guests, including Walt Disney during the making of one of his nature films, *One Day at Teton Marsh*. That summer a mock-up model of a beaver house occupied the living room of the main cabin where my sister once slept in her baby basket.

Struthers Burt, about 1915.

Katharine Newlin Burt, 1919. Publicity photograph for *The Branding Iron*.

Horace Carncross, the psychiatrist who delivered me.

Aunt Jean Burt.

"God and me made all this."
Nathaniel Burt, about 1915.

Cal Carrington in chaps.

The Countess in Camp.

Menor's Ferry, with Model T aboard.

Front of main cabin, Bar BC, Struthers Burt and Horace Carncross to left. Note sod roof.

Back of main cabin. Courtesy of George Vaux.

Diving board at the pool. Note female costumes, about 1915.

On the fence near the corral, about 1915.

Horses saddled and waiting, 1915.

Katharine Merritt, Helen Bispham, and friend leaving for Victor, Wyo., in the White Truck, about 1921. Courtesy of Virginia Huide-koper, Wilson, Wyo.

PART TWO: The Great Divide, 1930–1950

4.

UP ON THE CREEK

IN 1930 we moved from the Bar BC to the Three Rivers (so called because it was contained in a U formed by Pacific Creek, the Snake River, and Buffalo Fork). By that time both my parents had become very successful authors, my father as best-selling novelist (*The Interpreter's House*, 1924; *The Delectable Mountains*, 1927; *Festival*, 1931) and as a prolific writer of short stories and articles. My mother was a novelist, short-story writer, and creator of serials for women's magazines — the kind of profitable authorship that formed the basis of America's literary prosperity from 1900 till the era, beginning in the late 1950s, when mass-market magazines began to be killed off by television. Dude wrangling had become a time-consuming liability for them rather than a livelihood. With relief my father gave up the Bar BC and dude wrangling (or so he thought) and bought two small neighboring ranches twenty miles up the valley on Pacific Creek. Although the purchase was made in 1928, we all went to Italy in 1929, and it was only in 1930 that the Burts actually moved upstream permanently.

It was a tremendous wrench for all of us, but especially for my sister and me. It meant leaving Our Country, giving up our "inheritance," drastically reducing our scale of references, abdicating our claim to this imaginary Denmark-sized corner of Jackson Hole and assuming the much more modest and intimate occupancy of Pacific Creek Valley. The fact was that we were not really *in* the Hole any more, much less in the very center of it. Our new location was off to one side, subsidiary, suburban. The Tetons were now a faraway backdrop, not an overwhelming presence. The great skies, the great flats were reduced in compass to a cozy, hill-sheltered, segregated cup, a valley at the edge of the valley.

The new Three Rivers Ranch was composed of two older homesteads, the Snell place and the Arthur place. Pacific Creek is one of the sizable streams that come into the Snake from its northeastern flank—Pilgrim, Pacific, Buffalo Fork, Spread—most of them raging torrents in spring and reduced trickles in fall. Pacific Creek has a peculiar beginning far up in the wilderness at the south border of Yellowstone. A spring comes down from heights onto a high flat pass or saddle right on top of the Continental Divide. Here it slips out and down on *both* sides to form simultaneously Atlantic Creek and Pacific Creek. Atlantic starts off northwestward to flow eventually into the Gulf of Mexico—by way of the Yellowstone, the Missouri, and the Mississippi. Pacific starts off southeastward to flow into the Pacific—through the Snake and Columbia. Before Pacific Creek reaches our ranch, it goes through a modest canyon (heading more or less south), comes out into a sagebrush level still known as Ferrin Flats, then hits a ridge and is turned abruptly westward towards the Snake. Just before the junction, Pacific Creek makes a wide bend northwestward and back again—and in that curve nestled the Three Rivers. Low ridges cut the ranch off from the outside world, as represented by the main road to Dubois and Jackson, the post office of Moran, and the Snake River.

This Pacific Creek Valley, from the Ferrin Flats down to

the Snake, was once a small community of ranches. There was the Ferrin property, one of many of that family's big holdings, then the Braman place, still theirs and our only near neighbors, though separated by the wide wanderings of the creek. Lower down and on either side of the outlet of Two Ocean Lake was once the Thompson ranch. There are still signs of Thompson ditches and fences and cabin foundations; but the Thompsons were gone before we arrived.

Below us, and between us and the Snake, was the Hogan fox farm. This was an unpleasant neighbor. The foxes consumed old horses, and depots of smelly horse carcasses marred the Hogan approaches south of our ranch. In the thirties a fashion for silver fox furs made such fox ranches temporarily profitable. There was also Elk post office (this preceded the present Moran, which was then up under the shadows of the Jackson Lake dam) and the cabin of an eccentric Old Man Roudebush. He and Old Man Snell and Old Man Arthur— all such ancient recluses are always "Old Man So-and-So"— lived more or less side by side in Pacific Creek Valley. What did they think of each other? Were they friends or feuders? Nobody now knows. I recollect nothing of Arthur. Even the site of his cabin has disappeared.

Snell, a rather sinister and saturnine gentleman, was a refugee from the Johnson County cattle wars of the 1890s. As a supporter of the small cattlemen in their fight with the big ones, he one day received a warning, a human ear sent to him in the mail. He decided it was time to leave, and came to hide in this secret pocket along Pacific Creek. His cabin, a high-peaked 1900-looking structure, still stands; but I myself never saw either of our original Old Men, Snell or Arthur. The division, however, between the two ranches still existed when we first moved. The southern section, the Snell place, closest to

97

the main road and nestled under the ridge, is where we always lived. The Arthur place, north and bordered by the creek, became a hayfield.

The change of location meant a drastic change of scenery and in our feeling for place. Whereas the Bar BC included the Teton range and all its lakes, the great sweep of river and miles of flats in its prospect, we were now confined to this creek bottom and surroundings. It was far less grandiose and extensive, far more private and intimate, but still extensive enough by the standards of more settled places, since the Three Rivers itself comprised nearly three hundred acres and our "riding country" lay about us in a radius of a good five miles. Where at the Bar BC we had to cover leagues of sagebrush in dust and sun, or rain and thunder, to get to any sort of real scenery, at the Three Rivers we were nestled in the midst of an Eden that began right at our ranch limits.

Our front gate southward opened through a fence that ran along the crest of an open ridge. From the top of it there was a marvelous view up the Snake River valley west towards Jackson Lake, Mount Moran, and the whole line of the Tetons. Outside the gate a drive led for a mile or so to the main road, and the country round about opened first onto a long willow swamp and then rose to even higher ridges starred with various spectacular viewpoints looking down over the Hole. We immediately christened these crests with names of our own—Reed Ridge and Merritt Mountain—names of Three Rivers associates, names of which my father heartily disapproved, but which the rest of us found both handy and cozy. It was a tremendous convenience to say we were going to ride to Reed Ridge rather than trying an elaborate explanation of just exactly which promontory we had in mind.

Along down by the creek itself there were rides through

groves of great cottonwoods and spruce trees, and at least two semipermanent fords across into our other, northern riding country centered about the twin lakes, Two Ocean and Emma Matilda. This fantastically lovely and ridable landscape consisted of parks bordered by aspens interspersed with bare ridges or thick lodgepole forests. Though our new playground may not have been either as extensive or as grandiose as the foothills of the Tetons, it was infinitely more various and enticing to explore than anything close to the Bar BC. Before long this too became Our Country in a far more special and real way than the vast southward area had ever been.

"We" were also now a quite different group—no longer dudes, roughnecks, and owners, but the Associates, plus the foreman, cook, and the few summer hands that worked for them. Instead of really getting away from crowds and dude wrangling as he thought he meant to do, my father compulsively carried the atmosphere of a dude ranch with him.

Five families came up country, friends, some of long standing, all Easterners. Tucker Bispham and his wife Helen and their dog Jinks, a rather contentious airedale, were the oldest acquaintances, Tucker having been a collegemate of my father's and a fellow Philadelphian. He too was retiring from active participation in the running of the White Grass, though the Bisphams always kept a cabin there. Helen's friend, Katharine Merritt, a well-known pediatrician and daughter of Congressman Schuyler Merritt, of Stamford, Connecticut—for whom the Merritt Parkway is named—was another. Alan Reed, a business manager of the *Saturday Evening Post,* and his family —wife Katharine, daughter Mary Allison, son Alan, Jr.—were the very first to build their cabin and move in. George Amory and his wife Renée were also, like the Reeds, former Bar BC dudes. Halsey Malone, a New York lawyer and widower, with his son Adrian and his stepdaughter Elena de Struve, were exceptions, since they were friends of the Amorys, not of my father, and had not been his dudes.

The foreman was Frank Giles, rival of George Ross as guide on the Bar BC. He had a large family of various disposition and character. His wife, Emma, good housewife and faithful mate, was otherwise a difficult personality. She had a gnome-like look, a gruesome voice, and a constant and morbid delight in bloodshed, operations, and disasters, which she liked to share with the other female inhabitants of the ranch.

Of their many children, Francis, the oldest, had been the paragon—handsome, good, a fine hand. But he had died before the Gileses came to the Three Rivers. There were two other sons. The elder was Lamar, also a rather handsome but lachrymose young man, brought up under the shadow of paragon Francis, kind and amiable but somehow unfortunate in his efforts. He fought continually with his father, who was grimly dictatorial and censorious; and in fact Lamar was not the ranchman his father was or his brother had been. He made stupid mistakes. His father pointed them out to him scornfully. Lamar often as not burst into tears.

Lamar had a wife, Grace, dark-haired, plump, pretty, an Idaho village belle given to bouts of emotional upset, but fundamentally a jolly soul, who also fought with the senior Giles. There was a younger son, Victor, a humorous, lean adolescent with a sly charm, very handy with horses. He was of an age with Adrian Malone and Alan Reed, Jr. They made a threesome whose sporting activities did not coincide with ours. They did not participate very often in our explorations. The Gileses had numberless daughters with queer Mormon names like Melba and Greeba. Some of them were respectable matrons, some were very much not so; but Emma seemed to be equally proud of them whether they went straight or went wrong.

The kitchen was dominated by Pedro Rapatan, a nut-faced, dark-skinned, tiny Filipino. He had been a cook from time immemorial at the Bar BC and kept right on cooking for us into the 1960s—at least thirty-five years altogether. Like all old cooks, he was power mad and peculiar; but he loved us, particularly my father. He didn't care whether he was feeding three or thirty, and though not subtle, his food was always eatable. He had once had a wife, like Joe LePage, but during all the time we knew him he lived a bachelor life with obscure residences on vegetable farms in Utah or eastern Wyoming during the winter. He played the guitar, singing monotonous Tagalog songs, especially when moodiness seized him.

At such times he got drunk and, as a climax to these dark periods, would suddenly walk down the road carrying his suitcase, muttering and outward bound. My father would drive after him, pick him up, argue with him, console him, and invariably bring him back to the only real home he had. This was an annual occurrence. Waitresses came and went. If they were pretty girls, Pedro fell in love with them and treated them with Othello-like jealousy and tantrums. He once got a young fellow Filipino, named Narcis, to come to us for the summer. Narcis made inspirational mottoes that he framed and placed about the kitchen but fought with Pedro even more than the girls. Nobody, in fact, ever could work with him for very long without quarreling. Both Frank and Pedro had beautiful relationships with us and violently cantankerous ones with everybody else.

The great moment in all of Pedro's life occurred in September of 1933. A bear, refugee no doubt from Yellowstone, began raiding the garbage cans and storerooms back of the kitchen, tearing out the screen window and lapping up milk from the wide pans in which it was kept. He got to be an intolerable nuisance. We tried all sorts of ways to get rid of him. I remember one tense night with all of us hiding in the dark kitchen armed with shotguns full of rock salt and supplemented by Roman candles, tin pans, tin tubs, and other noisy paraphernalia. The bear came, we let loose with a frightful racket, the bear skedaddled—and came right back the next night. Pedro's outhouse (we all used outhouses then) was across the road, in trees, quite a walk from his kitchen bedroom. He and Narcis carried knives and finally guns for nocturnal protection against the bear.

Sure enough, not long after our session with the tin pans, Pedro met the bear at night on the way to the outhouse. In the dark he shot him and killed him. The next day proud pictures were taken of Pedro with gun in hand, the bear at his feet. Examination disclosed that the bullet had entered the bear's rump and traveled all the way to his heart. Otherwise we would have certainly been cookless. The bearskin hung for years on the wall of the main-cabin living room.

During the war Pedro composed ballads involving the supposed exploits of my brother-in-law, George Atteberry, and myself—naval aviator and communications officer respectively—and our supposed valiant work in liberating the Philippines. Since the ballads were in Tagalog and interminable, they were something of a trial to us; but they seemed to be complimentary in the extreme. The only words we could understand were our names, introduced here and there. In fact, Pedro could barely speak English. As he got older and deafer, communication almost ceased. He began to lose his recipes one by one, so that our meals became more and more limited and repetitious.

Finally he stopped cooking altogether, but lived every summer in a small cabin on the ranch, isolated by deafness and senility. He brought supplies from His Kitchen to cook for himself. One night he just curled up in his sleep and died. We never knew how old he was. He was buried in the Jackson graveyard, not far from my father, in the middle of a spectacular thunderstorm worthy of Beethoven's funeral. A few friends but no relations wrote to us afterward. He seemed to have no family except the Associates of the Three Rivers.

Unlike the dudes of the Bar BC, who came and went and were considered definite inferiors, the Associates of the Three Rivers were our beloved equals. In the never-to-be-repeated harmony of the first years, euphoria and companionship filled the atmosphere. Each partner built his own cabin, reflecting the differences of taste and personality. We all ate together in the splendid big main cabin decorated with Indian artifacts taken from the Bar BC.

The Reeds were all blond, good looking, hearty. Alan, Sr., had been very successful with the Curtis Publishing Company. Having had a vision, one day on the top of the ridge above his cabin, that he should get rid of his common stock, he reinvested his funds more securely. This was in 1929 and so, when the crash came, the Reeds were well fixed. Most unfortunately, Alan himself, a handsome big man, kindly but forceful, whom I barely remember, died almost as soon as the family moved to the ranch. His widow remained unconsolable; but, instead of taking her sorrow out in dark clothes and good works, she became more reckless, ostentatious, and spendthrift as the years went by. She turned from being a rather modest if genial housewife into a sort of mature rodeo queen who dressed in startling Mexican outfits, which did in fact become her outrageously, treating everyone at the local bars to drinks and drinking a good deal herself. Her children followed suit, not to their advantage.

Renée Amory, a lean, hook-nosed heiress who lived in a great chateau in Tuxedo, New York, in the winter, was always causing mild disturbances; but my father "new how to handle her," as Helen Bispham knew how to handle Tucker and his vagaries. Renée hated riding. Her avocation out West was housekeeping, which she never had a chance to do in the Tuxedo chateau. She also sunbathed. Her husband, George Amory, a big, modest, rather retiring gentleman, liked fishing, but he too was a sun worshiper. They both wore shirts of some special material that let in the sun through the cloth, and constructed a fancy, square, canvas sunbathing enclosure so that they could get tanned in the nude. Renée had a horse named Tuxedo, a spotted white roan plug that was the only horse she would ever ride. She had a saddle made with a soft quilted-leather seat, and occasionally took Tuxedo back East with her, where he lived in unhappy and lonely grandeur on the estate.

Halsey Malone, like George Amory, was another silent partner, as opposed to the very vocal Bisphams, Reeds, and Renée. He was a smallish man, with a quiet, dry wit, a widower whose late wife had formerly married a Russian diplomat. Their daughter Elena de Struve loved the ranch. She was handsome but plump, a disorderly dark girl, insanely devoted to animals. Her beloved pet was a mean milky-eyed Pinto named Nomad. She had a way of flinging her arms around his hind legs in a passionate embrace. If anyone else had tried that they would have ended up in the hospital. Adrian, Halsey's own son, was dark like Elena, silent and humorous like his father. He spent his time on horses with Alan and Victor, and we Burts didn't see much of him.

Katharine Merritt, our third "ranch Katharine," was very much part of our riding life. She was a pediatrician in New York, well known both as practitioner and teacher, a pioneer as a successful woman professional. Out West she liked to revert to an almost abject dependence on my father, who was always having to help her out of little quandaries with stoves and, later on, toilets. On the other hand, she was always being forced to doctor not only ranch people but ranch animals— most unwillingly but efficiently. Always handsome, if originally rather stern, she blossomed in later life into a real beauty, and still in her nineties remained one of the best-looking and best-dressed of white-haired women.

Bisphams, Burts, Katharine Merritt and her guests, usually English, made up the core of the exploration group. We were always out on picnics together into strange new areas, and we were the ones who named the landmarks roundabout. The Reeds rode for exercise and show. Their favorite jaunt was an open circle around by the outlet of Two Ocean that they called the Hangover Ride: therapeutic after a hard night in Jackson. Halsey and the Amorys seldom rode at all.

Despite differences in preferences and temperament, this original group was a very happy and congenial one. The partners all liked each other and looked on my father as chief, parent surrogate and dude wrangler. What with the Giles-family squabbles, Pedro's troubles with waitresses and problems of maintenance, however, my father found his time filled, and was really just as busy as he ever had been at the Bar BC. He did not get as much writing done at the Three Rivers as he might have; which was, subconsciously, pretty much his idea. He would do anything to put off settling down to the desk in the morning.

My mother wrote hard. The rest of us played. It was basically a simple, not to say still rather primitive life. When we first went up, there was no electricity or plumbing. There were wells at the main cabin, the Burt cabin, and the foreman's cabin, but they were always going dry or silting up. By 1933, year of the bear, we were in the grip of the Kohler. The Kohler was a gas-driven generator that was supposed to supply us with electricity. I always had hated the thought of electric lights as the first step of the intrusion of Civilization into our western life, quite rightly, in fact; but the Kohler was still a long way from true Civilization. It broke down continually, and at least once a summer absolutely. The only man who could fix Kohlers in the whole Intermountain Region seemed to be Van Arsdale. He traveled about a vast circuit repairing machinery, and paid for his visits by telling marvelously incredible stories. Gradually over the years electric lights superseded candles and lamps. Plumbing overcame outhouses and tin tubs. When the power line came up from Jackson after World War II, Civilization at last intruded fatally and finally. Life was certainly far more convenient and comfortable; but we lost something in isolation and freedom and the feeling of the frontier.

In the early days a good deal of the morning, especially for the ranch women, was spent in chores. I fetched water and chopped wood. I also grubbed sagebrush, an endless occupation, since the whole upper ranch where our cabins had been built was covered with this grey-green desert brush, which my father liked when it grew out on the flats but of which he greatly disapproved in the environs of a cabin being lived in. I also shot the chiselers that infested the sagebrush, scampering and chattering all over, tunneling the dryness with their complicated burrows and sitting upright at the edge of their holes to provide easy marks for me and my twenty-two. They were rather cute, but verminous, and were reported to be cannibals, feeding on their dead relations.

There was always an enormous amount of ranch work to do, though we raised no stock and didn't even grow vegetables. Horses had to be wrangled in and out every day, fences had to be kept repaired, ditches kept running. After awhile, Frank started a hayfield on the Arthur place, laying out ditches with Mormon skill, and he and Lamar and a team did all the work from spring irrigation to fall cutting and stacking. Horse-drawn machinery and family labor cost very little as compared to what has become an extravaganza of elaborate motorized mowers, rakers, balers, and gangs of hired labor. The process nowadays is far quicker and less laborious, but the difference in price is astronomical.

What most of us did, of course, was ride. What marvelous riding those first years provided, with everything new and to be discovered, few real trails, few outside intruders. My father had grown tired of riding, like most dude wranglers, though he still loved fishing. He also had developed some sort of leg trouble. He would occasionally take a group of us out on state occasions, picnics or tours, to show visitors the country. In the first days Frank also sometimes led us out; but mostly it was the core group of Bispham-Merritt-Burt who rode, or just my sister and myself; out every day and often all day.

There were two general provinces of country to be mapped, the area on the ranch side of Pacific Creek with its viewpoints and the area across the creek and about the lakes. There was also a rougher and more remote area into which we occasionally penetrated farther up Pacific Creek. The first country was delimited by the rather deep, rough gorge of Lava Creek and a high, bare hill we called Shell Mountain because of fossils we found on top. The other country across the creek was bounded by Pacific Creek very roughly to the east and south, and by a big hill, heavily timbered, on its southwestern flank that had already been officially christened Lozier Butte on the maps. Beyond the terminal moraines of the two lakes lay the wide-open flat valley of Pilgrim Creek more or less northward. We vainly tried to get Lozier called Burt Bluff, at least on the ranch, but we never had any success. It seemed unfair that the Reeds and Katharine Merritt should be memorialized and not us.

Within these two riding areas was (and is) a great variety of landscape — woods and parks and sagebrush flats, ponds and smaller streams, willow swamps, gorges. The two big lakes are glacial cups, long and not very wide, with low shores and no inlets. Being spring fed, their levels remain constant and the summer temperature very warm, quite unlike the snow-fed Teton lakes. We swam there and the Reeds even brought up a canoe. Both lakes had been dammed in a futile, petty fashion, but little if any damage was caused, since the dams were quite ineffective — just gestures towards vandalism and Progress.

When we first arrived in 1930, there were few real trails through this lake area, and it was the summer grazing range of a great elk herd. In fall, when the rutting season began, the whole tawny aspen-groved landscape was alive with bugling bulls and huddling cows, and we expected to see a dozen on any ride. There were also individual moose and small families of deer. Beaver abounded in the swampy outlet of Two Ocean and along Pacific Creek. Bird life of a rather special sort clustered about and on the lake, the usual ducks and geese and also seagulls taking a summer vacation from the Pacific and wild swans (not only the whistler but the rare and almost extinct trumpeter).[1]

Our rides were always not only explorations but game-sighting expeditions. After the comparatively empty world of the Bar BC, this paradise of open, smiling, flower-deep meadows; aspen clusters; dark but not endless forests of pine and balsam; lakes; ridges with views; sudden gullies and beaver swamps; flats and creek beds; and always in the background the snow-covered peaks of the Tetons was to adolescent horseback nature-lovers as close to paradise as the world can ever expect to come.

The great exploratory days were in the summer of 1931; the year 1930 was tentative. We were busy settling down. During 1932, I spent a summer in Austria studying music. After that things were never quite the same for us again. The country slowly changed, for one thing. All our riding area was included in United States Forest Service land, later the new Jackson Hole National Monument and then the Grand Teton National Park. The only road into it, besides our driveway, was a dirt track used by hunters and pack trippers that went up Pacific Creek, with a fork off to the then deserted Braman place. There were rough car tracks wandering up to the lakes, but nobody used them but fishermen. Then the government built a real road to Two Ocean Lake, modest, but to us a gross violation of the virginity of our wilderness. Then the Bramans moved back, built up their cabins and fences, and began to sell off lots to summer visitors. There are now some score of summer cabins up there, and though they are invisible and secluded, cars began to become increasingly evident. Hunting had previously been banned, not only as a matter of course by the Park Service but even by the Forest Service up Pacific Creek. When the Forest Service opened the creek to elk hunters, our

[1] There exists now a Trumpeter Swan Society with wide membership and annual conventions where the members get together and talk swan.

great elk herd vanished, going way up to safety beyond the hunting areas, even for the summer.

After World War II all these processes accelerated. The Two Ocean road has been "improved" and part of it even paved. Many trails are now cleared boulevards and strings of horseback tourists from the lodge, itself a monstrous modern intrusion, are occasionally met trailing after a bored wrangler. The aspen blight came along in the fifties, destroying the greenness and symmetry of the groves, now filled with downed timber and impenetrable to riders. Then the far more terrible pine-beetle blight devastated the lodgepole forests.

As for us, we grew up, were less easily overwhelmed by the excitements of discovery, and discovery itself became less and less possible. Eden faded, outside and inside, and became just the ordinary world, though a very specially beautiful world still, to be sure. Even the happy group at the ranch began to disintegrate.

But during the miraculous summer of 1931, untouched yet by the ominous outside events of the Depression and wars abroad, isolated from newspapers, the great park battle already almost won, or so we fondly hoped, the Burt youngsters flung themselves into nature worship. It is hard to recapture the intensity and vividness of that worshipful ecstasy. My copious diary records it in embarrassingly childish rhetoric.

Julie and I had brought with us favorite horses from the Bar BC. Mine was a stocky dark chestnut gelding with a blazed face named Euchre, sold to us by Bill Howard. Julie's was a pinto named, of course, Pinto. Later she exchanged him for a handsome black called Chris. His real, fancy name was Christophe, after the ruler of Haiti, an island in which my parents were much interested at the time. All three horses were marvelous trail horses, intelligent, sure footed, reliable. Euchre, however, was reliable only outside the gates. Once on the ranch he liked to indulge in fierce shies and sometimes ran with me in the hayfield. He always knew what he was doing and, though no doubt he hoped to throw me, it was all in sport, not panic or ferocity.

Julie on Pinto or Chris and I on Euchre rode out every day, often taking our lunches and sometimes coming in late for dinner. As the year advanced into fall, as the days grew shorter so that rides ended and climaxed with a sunset, as the leaves began to turn and the elk began to bugle and the harvest moon came up white and flat into the darkening of the east, our rides grew longer, our excitement more and more intense. This excitement built up towards a few memorable epic expeditions that I still recall as among the most vivid experiences of my life, of any kind.

The most memorable was in 1931, an exploratory trip around Two Ocean Lake. I was by myself and it was the first time that I had ever tried to go all around it.

It was September 25, and our last full day at the ranch for that summer. I started off in the afternoon with Katharine Merritt and her visiting friend, Josie Auchincloss. We went to the head of Two Ocean, riding along the open east side; then the ladies turned back home and I proceeded by myself. It had been snowing. The mountains were covered with white, and there were still patches of snow on the ground in sheltered places. We had seen no game, but had been hearing elk bugles. In the somewhat breathless prose of my diary:

I started up the gravelly trail that went up the ridge at the end of the lake. Aspens and a few firs on either side, and yellow grass meadows up the middle. The crest was bright with a mellow sun, and the trail led excitingly up ahead, through aspens into the sky. Bugling behind me now, crystal trumpets in the breathing quiet of the late afternoon. Finally emerged, as at the end of a crescendo, up on the long flat whitegrass fir bench. View of Sheep Mountain behind, very snowy. Caught the blaze of a trail on a big lone fir to the west and followed it. A bugle, now ahead. Across the flat and down the bench in trees by a well-marked trail, still wet with melting snow. Half way down I saw a big bull elk who had just finished bugling. I waited and saw him bugle again, lift his head back and call. Went down the trail as fast as I could walking, and came out on another flat, with the Tetons misty-milk-blue ahead. The bull was still there in plain sight with a herd of about fifteen. They got my scent and began to move south, in front of me. The bull bugled once or twice again, silhouetted against the far-away mountains, then ran with his now-frightened cows across the trail and into the woods up the hill. Went on down the trail, feeling very pleased and jubilant, especially as the others wouldn't come with me. I thought with malicious relish of what I would be able to tell them.

Finally in thick timber, reached the valley bottom and went for a way by the edge of Pilgrim Creek. Thick alder and pine half-swamp on my left. Came out on a sagebrush flat with a road running through it and over the creek by a wooden bridge. Kept close to the edge of the timber, and seeing a well-marked blaze on a tree, followed a trail into the cool and dark woods. Scared up a big bull moose, who ran off through the pines and alders. Came into a dark narrow meadow, its floor-level covered with whitegrass, and edged with willows. It came out at one end on the flat. High tree-covered bare-topped ridges ran along both sides. Straight ahead rose a tall mountain, black and pyramidal, capped with sun-lit red rocks and steeply covered with pine. It was a surprising and impressive setting for the bull moose who ran down the meadow away from me. Scouted around trying to find a definite continuation of my trail, but I couldn't, so went up the meadow toward the frowning height and attempted to get my bearings by climbing a sunny hill. I saw nothing except that it was getting late, so led Euchre down again into the cool and the shadow.

Heard a coyote howl just below me in a steep gulch. Crossed the head of the meadow in trees and hit a good trail going west in timber.

Coyotes howling close ahead. The trail went between ridges through a miniature canyon and split into three, one west, one southwest, and one south along the hill. Decided to follow the hill trail, though it wasn't a good choice. I went along among big firs and not too sure of where I was heading. The Tetons visible across a valley and ridges, and far away south, Jackson Lake.

Sunset beginning by now, and great red-moted shafts coming from the sun behind the Tetons. Trail quite smooth still, ahead of me, but wet and narrow and marked with the fleeing footsteps of my moose. Eventually came upon a valley that sloped east between the hills, narrow, dark and snow covered, but open. Followed it, but it ended dead in a gulch leading south and choked with heavy timber. So dismounted and led Euchre on a slippery and logged little game trail up the steep hill to the west. I'd just reached the level and mounted when I saw a coyote in the brush and, a few steps further on, standing against a lemon-colored sky, six or seven elk, fifteen feet away. They were led by a young bull, and when they got my wind turned and scampered down the steep slope ahead. I saw them running down the open into a gulch when I reached the crest of the hill. From there I saw the mountains again, blue, and the sky pale yellow behind them. A long fir hill, quite open, swept down straight before me and I followed it. I came upon a road and then the trail leading from it that went to the meadow on the west side of Two Ocean Lake.

I went along that trail, heading home, whistling and singing while the night came over me out of the east. Trotting through the big firs and the aspen, I caught sight of a huge white moon, low-rising in the southeast. It was so suddenly beautiful in the violet ashen sky, through the black branches, that I stopped. The mystery of the dusk and the ghostly beauty moved about me and there was bugling ahead in the meadows. When I reached them, the meadows were ringing with it, over towards the lake, and damning supper and the home-going trail, I left it and turned through a willow patch and some scattered pines to another meadow. Here I went walking Euchre and hoping to see a fight between some of the bugling bulls. What I saw was even more strange.

In the meadow ahead of me, in the woods along it, I saw and heard what must have been about twenty-five or more giant bull elk, wandering in the twilight. They were all old, from seven points on, so old the tops of their antlers were white. They were alone, no calves or young bulls, and they wandered around separately, bugling deeply and beautifully. The sky was dark now and the white, large moon lay in a pale amethyst-and-gray sky over the southern mountains. Behind me were the hills against the daffodil afterglow. I stood and watched this strange congregation, listened to such cascades of bugling as I have never heard . . . deep throaty brazen notes that rose up against the moon, fearful and exciting. One bull, seeing me, came running towards me, but seeing something unnatural about me stopped dead, puzzled. I moved towards him and he made off.[2]

I stayed there for a long while and finally in an ecstasy started home, as nearly as I could tell. It was dark now, or rather a strange twilight, half dusk, half moon. I went aimlessly through meadows, trotting and looking for a trail, but above all drinking in the evening. Stars began to bloom on the cobalt sky, the aspens died out like lamps. I saw vague flitting shadows that were elk, and heard an occasional bugling, clear in the stillness. Went up a dead-end valley once, and at last let Euchre more or less lead me. We crossed the Jackson Lake Lodge–Emma Matilda trail and Euchre took me down it, greatly relieved. The moon now was growing yellow, and threw occasional beams against the trunks of an aspen grove that looked like the light of a flashlight. A strange contrast, moon on one side, sun nearly gone on the other. I let Euchre carry me along, as night took complete possession. Passed a ruffled porcupine along the way. The aspens dark and wind-hushed, and stars all over the sky. Not a bit cold, but crisp and frosty. Cut across to the Two Ocean trail and the big meadow. It was glorious in the moonlight. Euchre wanted to go back the way we had come, but I took control and went straight along the trail, yodeling occasionally, thinking they might be out looking for me. Saw some elk running. They seemed floating patches of faint light silently and swiftly moving. Wind in the trees, stars. I thought I heard a voice (I cannot say "heard," for it was not received by my ears, but in my mind) saying, "It is the same, it is the same" (there is something else it is saying that I cannot fathom). "Fear and . . . ."

[2] This may have been a gathering of old bulls whose herds had been taken over by younger males, a sort of Senate of the Rejected. What exactly they were doing all together, I do not know.

I see! Fear and Beauty, Death and Life, Nothing and Everything, Night and Day . . . all these are the same, the complements of each other, the opposite sides of something that has no sides.

Home at last. Unsaddled Euchre and gave him a farewell hug. Ran up to the main house and to my amazement found them just finishing supper. I had thought it was at least nine o'clock. No search parties or bawlings out at all. Had supper, told my adventures.

Descriptions of rides tend inevitably to get fussily geographical. Descriptions of mystical experiences tend to get fuzzily lyrical. At best, seventeen-year-old prose is sticky; but the experience is there in essence. Whatever that Voice and its not very coherent message might have been, the pantheism of it was vividly real. "God immanent in Nature" was no more obvious to Wordsworth among his lakes than it was to me among mine. I have never quite repeated either the extraordinary vision of that congress of elk elders nor the intensity of that Voice. I have not been seventeen again. The word "unique," a nasty word and a tricky one, can perhaps safely be used here; the experience was unique for me, if not for others.

This kind of feeling in some fashion, this really religious feeling about wilderness, is what is back of much nature love and conservationism: it is the driving force, so to speak, behind National Parks and preservation efforts and such organizations as the Sierra Club and the Audubon Society and Wilderness Society. Those who fail to understand the fervidness of this religion don't realize what they are dealing with. What relation the faith has to art, on the one hand, and a true orthodox religion, on the other hand — not to mention politics, science and agriculture — I don't really know. It's a complicated equation. Much bad art, much spiritual heresy, I presume; but nobody who has not felt something of this kind of Pan-seeing can understand the depth and power of the love that some people have for the wilderness.

Back at the ranch, back at home base where dinner was being eaten without me, life was lived on a lower plane. While the Associates busied themselves with housekeeping and sun-bathing and fishing, like the Amorys, or dressing up in fancy outfits, like the Reeds, I occupied myself, when not on a horse, with what might be called undirected creative play. I wrote awful poems and improvised awful pieces on the piano and wrote fragments of awful novels and drew pictures just as I had as a child on the Bar BC. Instead of really immersing my-self in ranch activities and/or getting to know Jackson Holers of my own age, instead of really listening to and remembering the stories of my father's friends or becoming involved in the feckless pleasure seeking and love life of the Reeds and their guests and the younger dudes of the Bar BC, I was full of fantasies and philosophies, totally happy in my own imagina-tion and the adult protection and admiration of my parents.

It was not a very good preparation for life, depression, war, marriage, responsibility, or even real creative life; but it was a very delicious vacation dream world—that like all dream worlds seems to have to be paid for later on in terms of shocks of reality, just as the sweetness of life, the *douceur de la vie* of France under Marie Antoinette, had to be paid for by the Revolution. My dream world was, shall we say, somewhat less sophisticated, but it was equally removed from realities.

This dream world began to fade, as most dream worlds do, under the strain of inner tensions and outer distractions. When I left school at the age of sixteen, I decided to become a Great Composer. Though totally ignorant of music and completely untrained, I studied doggedly for two years in New York, went to college and left after my freshman year, studied some more, and at last began to discover that being a Great Composer was not quite as simple a process as I had imagined. Even summer in Wyoming was tainted with this disillusionment.

Meanwhile in the real world, which I so casually ignored and in which my father was so fiercely involved, all sorts of things were happening that were eventually to absorb even me. The park battle first came into the open in 1929 when the government created the Grand Teton National Park out of what had before been National Forest. The pro-park people now had a basis from which to work; the monument, however, was not created till 1943 and made into a park until 1950. It was battle all the way.

The fight against Prohibition was equally important to my father, and the election of 1932 very crucial. It was thought that Franklin D. Roosevelt would be as favorable to conservation as he was opposed to prohibition, though nobody seemed to know much about him. We all at least knew that local Republicans were violently against the park. These hopes for Roosevelt turned out to be correct. It was on these bases, prohibition and conservation, rather than on economics that my father was originally pro-Roosevelt. The depression did not affect the family; that is, my parents both continued to receive high prices from magazines and royalties from their books; but other Associates who lived on the stock market and investments—notably the Amorys, Bisphams, and Malones—felt the pinch.

From 1932 on, the rise of Hitler troubled and infuriated my father. He was heart and soul with Roosevelt in his internationalism and violently opposed to isolationism. Again, many Jackson Holers were not, and all through the thirties my father battled for conservation in the Hole, in particular, and the

New Deal and internationalism, in general. We children followed along with loud and passionate loyalty but, of course, could not do much about it except talk. There was no question in either of us of any "generation gap" as far as national and world affairs were concerned.

The outside world also impinged on us in a more direct way. Innumerable visitors came to the Three Rivers. Most were friends of my father; but many were long-staying guests of the other Associates. Some were purely political, like the almost annual influx of investigating senators. Into my own private dream world intruded those parental politics, the various visitors, adolescent social life — with residual connections to the Bar BC — Jackson and its rodeos and drinks and gambling, and the conflicts of growing up. It began slowly to occur to even me that I would have to do something, leave the nest, plan some sort of career; perhaps make a living! Voices at sunset never said one word about all that.

The Three Rivers Association that flourished so contently in 1930 began to dissolve in the middle of the decade. The first crack, the first defection, was caused by a dreadful accident that occurred in 1935. We were away again, as we had been in 1929, this time spending a foggy summer in Maine. One day Emma Giles appeared drooling with relish to inform the Associates that "Helen Bisham" had been "throwed and drug." Her horse had shied while she was out with Tucker in the area of Emma Matilda, she had been thrown, her foot had caught in the stirrup (low heels), and she had indeed been dragged and badly injured.

This kind of sudden and terrible accident, always a desperate element of ranch and Western life — my sister, aged nine, had been kicked by a horse on the Bar BC, her skull fractured, and she almost killed — has been a recurrent pattern through all my Western experience. In this particular case it began the break up of the first Association. When Helen recovered, she didn't want to ride any more. The Bisphams decided to go back permanently to their cabin at the White Grass. As the oldest and best friends of both the Burts and K. Merritt, this was a dreadful blow. Nobody, least of all my father, had ever really thought through what would happen if partners dropped out. Who owned the cabins, the partners or Old Man Ranch? Who was to pay the missing yearly maintenance, which though pitifully small in those days was still very crucial, since it alone supported the ranch? This was all supposed to be covered in a semimythical and extremely vague set of principles called the Gentlemen's Agreement. According to this unwritten and extra-legal constitution, any Associate who wanted to retire was supposed to keep on paying maintenance until such time as said Associate could find a substitute to take his place — a substitute perfectly agreeable to *all* other Associates. The fantastic difficulties of fulfilling this obligation — and the basic fragility of all such cooperative ventures (youth communes and religious fraternities please take note) — now suddenly became very clear. An association of affluent people with long mutual dude-ranching experience and friendship with my father in 1928 was a different matter from a mid-Depression attempt to find someone suitable to take the place of the Bisphams in 1936.

There was, of course, no real equity involved. The ranch had been acquired in good faith by my father for a few thousand dollars just at the time that land was being bought by Rockefeller for a future park. My father had not realized that the Pacific Creek Valley and its lakes were included in the planned park boundaries. When he found that they were, he believed that, as a prime mover in the park project and John

119

D. Rockefeller's scheme to buy land for it, he was honor bound to sell his property to Rockefeller rather than allow his enemies to accuse him of "profiteering" on the basis of inside knowledge. So we ended up on a government lease with my father as sole lessee, and there was no question of the partners being part owners of real estate. All they really possessed was the furniture in their cabins and a sort of theoretical membership in the Association, to be sold for whatever they could get for it from a prospective substitute partner.

The Bisphams had no ideas about such a substitute and made no efforts to get one. My father and Katharine Reed did find somebody — a hard-riding, hard-drinking, very amusing, very rich couple called Brown, residents of suburban Connecticut but of Californian and Hawaiian background. Mrs. Brown's first name was Aloha and she did a mean hula. Though the more sober members of the community, notably K. Merritt and the Malones, took a dim view of the Browns from the start, everyone wanted to oblige the Bisphams and help the ranch. The Browns were admitted with much lavish party giving and proceeded to redecorate the Bispham cabin with trophies of foreign travel and high living.

Unfortunately after this splendid beginning everything went downhill. The Browns became interested in another ranch elsewhere and came less and less to the Three Rivers. Paul Brown and my father fought. Before the end of the decade he offered the Browns a nominal sum for their cabin and they left never to return. Katharine Reed also got involved in a project for a cattle ranch down country. She became progressively alienated from the rest of the Associates and at one point she refused to eat with the rest of the group in the main cabin. She set up her own kitchen, cook, and food-supply system, all of which caused conflicts with Pedro. Drinking and carrying on became obnoxious and flagrant.

Another cause of friction was the whole area of public affairs. Not only were the Reeds violently anti-New Deal Republicans but they were pro-Hitler. Katharine had a sister married to a Munich industrialist who thought Hitler was wonderful. The Burts did not care for this. Eventually Katharine also fought with my father, left the Association, and, like Brown, was paid off for her cabin and share. So much for the Gentlemen's Agreement. World War II finished off the already decadent first Association. Halsey Malone died without making any particular arrangements for continuing his ranch partnership. The Amorys pulled out, amicably but finally. By the time the war was over, there was nobody left but the Burts and Katharine Merritt.

I spent my last prewar summer at the Three Rivers in 1937. After that I was too busy with my own life to do more than make short visits. Then came the war. Paradise, that adolescent Arcadia of unexplored country, youthful ecstasy, the whole romance of our second Western kingdom, was pretty well liquidated. When I came back after the war, it was all Real Life with a vengeance.

Burts on horses, early 1930s: (from left) Nathaniel Burt, Struthers Burt, Katharine Burt, Julia Burt

Frank Giles. Note brand-new main cabin and pool behind, about
1930.

Main cabin and Tetons from Reed cabin.

Katharine Reed in drinking costume with friend.

Pedro.

5.

THE PARK

THE year 1930 was not only a break in the Burts' private life, it also marks a watershed in the history of the valley. Perhaps the year is even a watershed in the history of the Far West as a whole. The Northwest—that is, the northern Far West, not the Pacific Northwest—is such a young country as far as permanent white settlement is concerned that even a decade can form an epoch in its history.

Until 1870 everything is really prehistory—Indians, trappers, travelers to the Coast. The first really permanent settlement in Wyoming was that of cattlemen after the Civil War. Then followed the great cattle boom of the open range and its collapse in the blizzard winter of 1887-88. This ruined many of the large owners, including Theodore Roosevelt, and put an end to what he and his friends, Owen Wister and Frederic Remington, always thought of as the Old West. *The Virginian*, of 1902, is a nostalgic record of that first period of Wyoming settlement and history. Jackson Hole played no real role in this first phase of Wyoming history. It was never a place for big cattle outfits, anymore than it had been a place for true Indian settlement. There were in fact no permanent settlers before 1880, and only a few before 1890. True occupation does not begin till after 1900.

It is during the second span of the history of the Old West

(from 1900 to 1930) that Jackson Hole took form as a community. The Hole was still very much frontier, remote from outside contacts, looking and acting in the pattern of *The Virginian*. There were, of course, dudes; but then there had been dudes like Owen Wister all through the West from 1870 on. The first dude ranch, that of the Eaton brothers, had been founded in the 1880s. This second span of the Old West, truly the last of the American frontier, except for Alaska, was the time of my father's active ranching career and of my idyllic Bar BC childhood. The Old West was very real indeed in the valley during all that time, though New Yorkers persisted in believing otherwise—as they have since the 1640s no doubt.

The period between 1930 and 1950 marked the change of Jackson Hole and, indeed, most of the Far West from Frontier to Region. Until then the West was full of pockets of real pioneering, places where technology had not penetrated, where electricity and plumbing and even automobiles were almost unheard of—a horse-drawn world. All these things, and innumerable other evidences of urbanization and sophistication, emerged during these twenty years of transition from 1930 on. Since the end of World War II the West and the Hole have been as characteristic as ever, but characteristic in a modern way—regionally characteristic as New England and the South have long been characteristic, but not peculiarly characteristic as Frontier.

These changes were already begun in the later twenties. A Bar BC dude, Lee Butler, made the first trip from the East to the Hole by automobile in 1928. I can still picture, in my mind's eye, a yellow convertible as the vehicle in question. Perhaps it's just a dream. In about 1927 when the nasty Elbo was founded, Wallace Beery, then famous as a movie character actor, flew into the Hole in his private plane, landed in the sagebrush on the flats, stayed at the Elbo ("Home of Hollywood Cowboys"), and chased the cook lecherously around the kitchen. He settled as a permanent touch of Filmland along Jackson Lake. The various dance halls at Jenny Lake and outside of Jackson were dependent on reckless and often disastrous automobile transportation for existence. Despite the dreadful roads of the twenties, more and more tourists infested them.

As far as the Hole is concerned, however, the Great Divide, the momentous change, was occasioned by the founding of Grand Teton National Park. Before 1930 the Hole was a self-sufficient and quarrelsome private entity. Since then it has really been an appendage of Uncle Sam. The movement that led to the establishment of the park was almost entirely a local conception; that is, the men and woman who first thought of the idea and worked to realize it were citizens of Jackson Hole, not outsiders. Jack Eynon, Joe Jones, Dick Winger, Maud Noble, Si Ferrin, and my father were among the Founding Fathers (and Mothers). Horace Albright, superintendent of Yellowstone and later director of the Park Service, was the only outsider importantly involved at the start, and his objectives —extension of Yellowstone, in particular—were often in conflict with those of the Jackson Holers.

The movement for "park extension," as it was inaccurately but usually referred to in those days, was supported by some local ranchers, all conservationists, and most enlightened visitors; but it was violently opposed by Jackson businessmen and many ranchers and even dude-ranch owners. The opposition was fundamentally based on plain instinctive hatred of govern-ment encroachment. The support was based on equally in-stinctive hatred of commercial encroachment.

The West has always been the victim of such encroachments, either of Big Government or Big Business. The latter has almost always been accompanied by all sorts of outside depredations and inside corruptions. From the very beginnings in the fur trade, rich Easterners or speculative foreigners have devised vast and often profitable schemes of exploitation, raping one natural resource after another — fur, gold, timber, oil, now strip-mined coal — and then leaving exhausted areas of exploitation to lapse back into somewhat tarnished wilderness. The by now picturesque ghost towns all over the West are testimony to these continuous programs of exploitation. The present coal and oil-shale boom is just the latest and most destructive of such depredations.

These grand operations have been supplemented by smaller ones, local hustlers anxious to make a quick buck, traders who sold whiskey to Indians, bankers interested in real-estate spec-ulations. Neither the large nor the small schemes are or have been necessarily or totally nefarious. Gold and copper, oil and timber are things people want and need. Water power and irrigation and Idaho potatoes and places to live are all in them-selves innocuous or beneficial. It is just that in most of these schemes, big and small, no account has been taken of other values, particularly the imponderables of scenic beauty, natural balances, the whole world that has now become fashionably publicized as Ecology. In these earlier days it was Conserva-tion, and was the cause of only a happy few, who did lonely and valiant battle with the huge forces of ignorance marching under the banner of Babbitt-like Progress. In 1930, with the rather spectacular collapse of Progress in the Depression, people in general were just beginning to listen to the voices of Conservation.

Jackson Hole, even from early days in the history of its settlement, was exploitable and exploited. The first Jackson Lake dam was built as early as 1904. When it washed out in 1910, the second and present dam was built during 1910 and 1911. For years and years afterward Jackson Lake was a horror of dead timber all along its shores and unsightly mud flats at its far shallow end. The dam itself was a violation, an invasion of the wilderness, and though time and effort have now toned down the rawness and cleaned up the mess, Jackson Lake is still not the beauty spot it was or might have been, beautiful as it now is. Of course Idaho potatoes, which are raised on water from the dam, are very nice things.

The Jackson dam was, at least comparatively, an honest outrage. Not so some other schemes. One dilly involved, as of the midtwenties, a complicated series of swindles. First other remaining undammed Teton lakes like Leigh, Jenny, and Taggart were to be impounded and ruined. The flats were to be irrigated and homesteaded by bewildered and ignorant would-be farmers. It would soon become obvious that the cobblestone flats were not farmable. The farmers would go bankrupt. Thereupon their land would become available to already resident ranchers, cheap and without their having to go to the trouble of homesteading. Since my father was one of the closest of these resident ranchers, he was among those propositioned. He saw to it that publicity killed the proposition.

There were many such ideas floating around, large and small. Already by 1930 gas stations and tourist camps were beginning to infest the still-primitive road toward Yellowstone. The dance hall at Jenny Lake and the Elbo, home of Hollywood Cowboys, and its rodeo grounds out on our flats were merely the most obnoxious and conspicuous eyesores. It became obvious to farseeing conservation-minded local people that frontier isolation was ending and that exploitation was imminent.

Already in my father's novel, *The Delectable Mountains*, the ravaging of a fictional country by a dam is described and deplored. To those like my father and his friends who loved the country as they had first known it, but who recognized that the tourist was coming, some sort of special preservation scheme was imperative. Letting human nature take its course meant ruin.

The most obvious move was to extend Yellowstone to include the Tetons. This idea had been discussed but usually rejected from the earliest days. In 1917, Horace Albright proposed such a scheme in his first annual report as acting director of the brand new (1916) Park Service. But nobody in the Hole wanted it to be just another Yellowstone, full of fat ladies from Kansas in knee britches, golf caps, silk stockings, high heels and lace blouses—this being the special traveling costume of the fat female tourist of those good old days. The spectacle of Old Faithful ringed by gum-chewing kiddies and of the concessionaire grand hotels of the park filled with motley hordes was not what anybody in Jackson Hole, least of all my father, wanted to see.

The idea was to preserve Jackson Hole, even the town of Jackson itself, as it was and had been, to preserve it as a tourist attraction perhaps, but not just as a tourist carnival. Some sort of effort like that of Colonial Williamsburg, in Virginia, was vaguely in mind. Jackson in those days was still an almost perfect specimen of a Western town like those already beginning to be seen in the movies and to be thought of as picturesque (Wister, far from thinking them picturesque,

132

thought all of them loathsome messes). Unpainted false-front stores and saloons, dusty streets with board sidewalks lined with hitching posts and rails to which horses and wagons were still hitched—this was Jackson until the end of the twenties and the onslaught of the automobile. Why not keep the valley and even the town exactly as it was? A "museum on the hoof" was, I believe, the phrase used by Dick Winger.

There was that famous meeting of the Founding Fathers at Maud Noble's cabin, at Menor's Ferry, in 1923. The local conservationists had Albright down to discuss plans. Park Extension was what Albright proposed, but it was not what the Founding Fathers wanted. Something on the order of a "Wild Life Williamsburg" gradually emerged as a possibility. But how to effect it? Was there any similar billionaire who might be interested? How about John D. Rockefeller, Jr., himself? None of the Jackson Holers knew him, but my father had been a winter resident of North Carolina, which is next to Virginia, and somewhere along the line he had made the acquaintance of Kenneth Chorley, Rockefeller's right-hand man in the establishment of the Williamsburg restoration.

As early as December 21, 1925, the Chorley diary mentions a lunch in New York with my father and a Fred Allen,[1] during which the scheme for saving Jackson Hole was discussed. Another entry of March 9, 1926, is more explicit:

At one o'clock went to lunch at the Coffee House with Mr. Allen and Struthers Burt. Mr. Allen was sick and could not be there. Struthers Burt wanted to talk to me about the proposed Indian Survey and then he talked to me a long time about the question of Yellowstone and acquiring some additional land. There is a good deal of opposition to this on the part of the natives of Wyoming. There has been Congressional investigation about it and everything

[1] I cannot seem to find out who Allen was. Chorley did not remember him.

else. It is very likely that a small range of mountains just at the northwestern corner of the Park will be taken over by the Park . . . this year, but he wants to see the whole of what is known as Jackson Hole Territory made a part of the Park. He says there is nothing else like it in this country. It is simply an outdoor natural history museum. He said the whole thing could be bought for a little over $1,000,000, and he is very anxious indeed for me to see Albright, who is the Superintendent of the Park, while I am out West this summer and talk the matter over with him. He is also extremely anxious for me to go down and see his ranch, which is just south of the Park. He is going to write to his partners and also Albright about my coming out there.[2]

Chorley did go west in 1926, and so did John D. Rockefeller, Jr., who was taken about by Albright and subjected to lots of quiet propaganda. Rockefeller had first visited the park in 1924. He had already been involved in buying land for the Park Service on Mount Desert for the future Acadia National Park and was interested in a scheme of road beautification in Yellowstone. When Albright took Rockefeller down through Jackson Hole in the summer of 1926, the message was communicated without Albright's having to say very much. JDR saw the Tetons and also saw the devastated shores of Jackson Lake and the Jenny Lake dance hall. The seed was planted; but the first planting was certainly that original lunch in December of 1925.

Though my father seems to have stressed Park Extension in his talks with Chorley, that was not what he really wanted. My diary of October 18, 1930, gives a truer picture: "Home just in time for supper with Mr. Eynon, Dick, Mrs. and Louise Winger as guests. Afterward great talk on the subject. Dick's new plan of a Wilderness (or Recreation) Area administered

[2]From the private papers of Kenneth Chorley, in possession of his widow and deposited at the Rockefeller Foundation.

by the Park, but a totally new thing; neither National Park nor Monument. No 'improvements' of any kind." This was what the natives really wanted, not just Park Extension. Could it ever have been realized? The present-day Wilderness Area legislation is close; but this plan of 1930 involved settled country.

The most honest and disinterested opposition to any sort of government encroachment, especially park extension, came from ranchers who had had lots of experience with bureaucratic interference and didn't like it. Wyoming was already half government property — in the form of public lands, Forest Service lands, Indian reservations, National Parks — and the resentment of Wyoming citizens against any further increase of public holdings is quite understandable. It was clear, however, that only the United States government in some form was fit to administer any sort of Jackson Hole Preserve. It was the only power big enough to resist local pressures, and the Park Service was the only agency totally committed to preservation and recreation. However distasteful Yellowstone might be, something of the sort was inevitable if the Hole was to be saved at all.

The sequence of events has often been told — the story of Albright's trip with Rockefeller, how in secret a Snake River Land Company was formed by Rockefeller's administrators, including Chorley, and how it began to buy up lands in the area of a proposed park, exactly as my father had originally proposed.

Most unwisely the first man chosen as purchasing agent was Robert Miller, the local banker. Miller was the second permanent settler in the Hole as of 1883 and founder of the town of Jackson; but he was a confirmed anticonservationist and lover of Progress. He welcomed the opportunity, as banker, of making good his bank's delinquent mortgages. Farmers and ranchers had been in a bad way even before the Depression, in fact ever since the collapse of the wheat boom after World War I. Once Miller had accomplished his purpose, he resigned and became a violent and outspoken opponent of "park extension," an especially dangerous enemy, since he knew all about the Rockefeller plans from the inside. Any one of the Founding Fathers could have, and no doubt did, tell the Rockefeller people that they had chosen the wrong man: they found it out the hard way.

Dick Winger succeeded Miller as agent; but a good deal of damage had already been done. The secret of Rockefeller money behind the sinister and mysterious Snake River Land Company ceased to be secret. The name Rockefeller had always stood for everything nefarious and Eastern and monopolistic in the West, and the opposition was joined by people on that basis alone. The prejudice still exists, as can be seen in Frank Calkins's otherwise fair-minded history of the Hole. The fact is, of course, that some secrecy was essential if prices were not to be driven sky high; and if there ever was an altruistic gesture, the purchase of land by JDR was in its origin. But for more than twenty years, until the final establishment of Grand Teton National Park with its present boundaries, the battle dragged on and on and on.

Nothing, of course, could be done by Wyoming opponents about the original transfer of Forest Service lands to the Park Service in 1929, which saved the actual Tetons from harm. It was the floor of the valley, the foreground of the panorama, that was the area of dispute. By 1933 the Rockefeller purchases were more or less complete: 35,000 acres at a cost of some $1.4 million. An extension of Grand Teton, rather than

Yellowstone Park, was now feasible; but opposition was so active and entrenched that nothing could be done.

Finally Rockefeller became disillusioned. He threatened to dispose of his rejected gift by public sale. This forced the Department of the Interior under Harold Ickes to put pressure on the president. Roosevelt used, or abused (according to his enemies), his powers to create a Jackson Hole National Monument in 1943. Only Congress could create a park, but a president could set aside sites of "historical" interest as monuments. Usually these were small areas that included battlefields or antique buildings. The proclamation of this enormous monument created an uproar. A special bill was proposed by Wyoming Congressman Frank Barrett to disestablish the monument, but it never became law. At last, in 1950, after the death of FDR and when the partisan politics of his regime had simmered down a bit, the monument was finally allowed to become part of the Grand Teton National Park. Fortunately, my father was still alive to enjoy his triumph. It had been a seemingly endless battle.

The uproar and oratory during this whole twenty-five years of struggle was tremendous and continuous. Old friends refused to speak to each other, everybody took sides. Congressional investigations that combined business and pleasure for the Solons had begun, as the Chorley diary makes clear, even before the battle was really underway. In the fall of 1933, for instance, a large delegation of senators descended and we lunched them at the Three Rivers. What a gallery of character actors! Senator Norbeck, of South Dakota, played the role of pioneer buffalo—rough, tough, growling in his moustache; fortunately, he was a friend of conservation, as he would have made a formidable enemy. By contrast, slim "Dapper Dan"

Nye, of North Dakota, wore, if I really remember correctly, a straw boater and natty tan business suit. He should have carried a cane. He could have joined George M. Cohan on stage singing "Yankee Doodle Dandy." Most flamboyant of all our lunch guests was Senator Ashurst, of Arizona. He affected the dress of the 1860s—a long black frock coat, shoulder-length hair, and a string tie. He insisted on making a speech about his little ol' mother defending herself in her cabin against Injuns. In between he fondled Katharine Reed's knee. Before he left he inscribed his name with a flourish on the dining room table, expecting that we would preserve it forever under glass. I wish we had.

A lesser "investigation" by Wyoming politicians—all, of course, good friends of my father but committed to the state's antigovernment position—took place on August 14, 1931, in Jackson. My diary of the next day records what my father told us about it:

Daddy came back for supper just a little before the first bell, bubbling with news. He got down to Jackson last night and saw all his old friends, had supper, and went to the place where the meeting was called. Senator Kendrick got up and said, "We (Senator Carey, Congressman Carter and myself) have been appointed as a committee to investigate this matter [the park, of course] in an open meeting. The proponents of the scheme will have thirty minutes to speak, then the opponents, with rebuttals on both sides." Dick Winger got up, made a very impassioned speech, not only because he was sick but also because he saw it was a frame-up, which it was. He knew that the whole senatorial delegation had been spending the afternoon with Bob Miller, the archenemy of the whole scheme. Then Bill Simpson got up and spoke. He's a little man who hunches his shoulders up and turns his head around him like a snake waiting to strike. He too made a very impassioned speech, full of misstatements, against everything of course. Then Daddy got up, having made notes of Simpson's lies on an envelope, and said, "Senator, may I ask Mr. Simpson some questions?" Simpson absolutely refused to answer. He said, "I came here to make a speech for the side on which I stand, and I will not be cross-examined. Who is this gentleman may I ask?" Senator Kendrick said, "O, I thought you gentlemen knew each other. Mr. Simpson, my old friend Struthers Burt, a resident of this valley for twenty years," at which everyone in the audience burst out laughing, as Bill Simpson has been writing bitter attacks on Daddy for a year. Well, finally Daddy sat down amid a great uproar, Simpson refusing to answer any questions, and after a short rebuttal, all three, senators and congressman, got up and made three of the most long and vicious attacks on the whole scheme possible and closed the meeting. Thus they hope to save their faces with the rest of Wyoming, which is against the park, at the expense of Jackson Hole.

This not very impartial account reveals the climate of opinion about "park extension" and the battles for and against it. As can be seen, Simpson was not one of those who remained my father's personal friends while being political enemies. Kendrick and Carey, on the other hand, did. When Simpson's son Milward became governor of Wyoming, he continued his father's battles against conservation with added effectiveness. I can't say I did more than just root for my father's side.

I wish I could remember the Founding Fathers better. Dick Winger outlived them all, and of course I recollect him well — a tall, lean, cadaverous, frequently ailing man with a caustic and marvelous sense of humor and a rather jaundiced view of human nature based on long Jackson Hole experience. He could almost have been typecast as the "Western-frontier-lawyer-editor" that in fact he was.

Joe Jones and Jack Eynon died earlier. I remember Eynon, a rancher, as a dark mountainous man, slow and rather silent.

139

Joe Jones was large too but not as mountainous, with curly reddish hair. At this time he was a Jackson storekeeper, but previously he had been a professional gambler and wrote his experiences for the *Saturday Evening Post* in 1923. He came to the Hole in 1907 as a homesteader and endured five years of incredible hardship trying to farm on the Grovont, also memorably described in the *Post*. He too, like all these men, was a marvelous storyteller, but all I can recollect was his statement that an expert, honest gambler could always outplay and detect a dishonest one. He knew all the tricks himself and gave us a pack of cards with subtle markings on the back. You would have had to have very good eyesight to cheat with those cards. He described all sorts of other devious devices, all of which I have forgotten now.

What grieves me most is having forgotten a lot of those wonderful stories, endless specimens of Far Western art usually based on the infinite eccentricity of human nature on the frontier. They rumbled through long evenings by our fireside without ever being tedious. They took the kind of listening appreciation for leisurely monologue totally alien to modern urban backchat. From the sober beginnings of "When I was down in . . ." to the intricate and fantastic denouement half an hour later, they were of a kind that seems to be obsolete. At least I haven't heard anything quite like them since. If only I'd been an adolescent tape recorder!

On that same dinner night of October in 1930 when Eynon and the Wingers talked about *the* subject, my diary records: "After, stories, Jack Eynon's of Wells's 'runaway': 'Reached down . . . grabbed the babby . . . My God Jack . . . it was . . . pitiful.' Really a masterpiece of comic art when he told it." Dick Winger had a wonderful story about a camp cook and canned peaches: "You take them peaches, Mister Winger, ..."

That is about all that is left me of those masterpieces of comic art; though I wonder whether they could be recorded properly in cold print anyway.

The man who has outlived everybody, Horace Albright, was a very different sort of man, not a "Westerner" in the sense of Eynon or Jones, though born in California. He has had ample, perhaps too ample, justice done to his tenacious and eventually successful efforts to see the park through. He was invaluable when the battle shifted to behind-the-scenes congressional Washington. But except for the constant references to that supposedly epochal meeting at the Noble cabin, which was in fact a sort of failure, and occasional mention of my father's role as publicizer and conservationist, the role of the Jackson Holers, the true Founding Fathers, has not been properly recognized.

Twenty years is a long time in the West. The Rockefellers and their fine work and the fine work of the Rockefeller assistants keeps green, but the kind of toughness and fighting spirit and imagination that it took for people who actually lived in the valley to envisage the whole idea, and then see it through against the bitter opposition of their friends and neighbors, certainly deserves more than the footnote it gets nowadays. Many of the worst enemies of the park in those days have now become its best friends, especially the Jackson bankers and businessmen whose fortunes have been made by the tourism the park brought in. Many of the people, or the kind of people (conservationists and wilderness lovers), who were such violent supporters of park extension have now become critical and disillusioned.

It was a famous victory all right; but like every other victory it has its bitter aftertastes. Though Grand Teton Park has an atmosphere all its own, which is quite different from that of

141

Yellowstone and far less monumentally mob oriented, it is still a big, famous, modern, popular, typical national park. It is not the special sort of preserve my father and Winger hoped for, a "museum on the hoof," or anything of the sort. The town of Jackson does not resemble Williamsburg and is as honky-tonk a tourist trap as any entrepreneur could desire, a city of neon-lit motels and Japanese curios—and also, it must be admitted, nice restaurants and art galleries.

Perhaps the bitterest aftertaste of all has been the development of Rockefeller interests, by his children, in the park itself. What could be more like a big, vulgar, concessionaire, Yellowstone hotel than the Rockefeller Jackson Lake Lodge? Just the kind of "improvement" we had all hoped to avoid. Then the fact that the Rockefeller family itself bought and kept the old JY Ranch, scene of my father's first Jackson Hole experiences, instead of selling it to the Snake River Land Company as my father sold his ranch—this too has not been popular. At the time they bought it, it was not to be included in the future park; and one can say they have certainly deserved well of the valley and ought to be expected to have some reward besides just surly thanks. But still, it's an aftertaste.

When my father (in the original spirit of altruism) sold his just-purchased Pacific Creek ranch for what he paid for it, he thereby deprived his heirs (that is, my sister and me) of at least a million dollars worth of real estate and the right to live and die on our own property instead of facing eviction when the fifty-year lease was up in 1979. My father complacently assumed that of course our lease would be renewable. He forgot that in fifty years everyone he knew would be dead, and that government agencies have very short memories indeed.

The Jackson Lake Lodge and its sister ship—the smaller and more exclusive Jenny Lake Lodge, a former dude ranch—and the Colter Bay area camp, all Rockefeller projects, are certainly models of their kind. But it is of a kind that the original proponents of park extension did not want—necessary and useful as they now are. The JY Ranch is well kept and in good hands; but private holdings of that kind in the park were not supposed to be encouraged. The park administration itself has been pretty model too; but the erection, for instance, of a colony of New Jersey development ranchers down by the Ferry in full view of all who come and go by the road, along with a massive garage right at the entrance of the Frew's beautiful 4 Lazy F . . . well, did it *have* to be done that way? So there has grown up a sort of backlash of antipark feeling among those who love Jackson Hole best, and a regret that something more on the order of Dick Winger's special creation wasn't possible.

Meanwhile, the old enemies of the park are riding the profitable bandwagon of unlimited tourism with high hearts and open palms. It was a famous victory and the Hole was saved from a fate worse than death, and, if the valley isn't the remote frontier valley my father saw in 1910, it at least is not the hideous scrambled egg of commercialism and crud that it would have been if the park had not come in. The modern development of the south end of the valley gives some idea of what this "crud" can be. On the other hand . . .

6.

THE FAST SET

DURING this period of transition from 1930 to 1950 the Hole was a curious and sometimes rather raucous blend of the old and the new, the primitive and the up-to-date. It was no longer a question of a few very sophisticated dudes in a very primitive frontier community. It was rather, a lot of miscellaneous new people in a community that was rapidly becoming pretty sophisticated itself. The Jackson Hole described by my father in the *Diary of a Dude Wrangler* gave way to the Jackson described by Donald Hough in *Snow Above Town* or *Cocktail Hour in Jackson Hole*. My father's book was essentially about ranches. Hough's books were about town life.

The town of Jackson, the only real center within a radius of about a hundred miles in any direction, had already by the 1930s evolved from a quiet, dusty cowtown towards a Tourist Mecca and center of Nite-Life. There had always been Saturday after-dark festivity and the rodeo was always a Saturnalia. During the thirties, however, the town began to take on a special lurid picturesqueness it never had before or has had since. Bars were more wide open and always included busy but illegal gambling establishments in the rear, and instead of going downtown for gaiety once or twice a year, as we did from the Bar BC, the Reeds and often the younger Burts and their Three River guests hardly missed a weekend during the summer.

144

As far as I myself was concerned, the climax of such night-life occurred during the summer of 1938. From 1930 through 1937 the whole Burt family had been on the Three Rivers from June to October. The exceptions were my trip to Austria in 1932 and the family residence in Maine in 1935. In 1938, I spent the first summer of my life on a ranch not family owned and run. I was a so-called dude wrangler on the Bispham-Hammond White Grass Ranch. Dude wranglers of that kind were and, I guess, still are youths who got and get free bed and board in exchange for their efforts to entertain dudes, particularly and inevitably younger female ones. There was a slight tinge of the gigolo about it.

I was of course not all that youthful, being twenty-four, and I took my job fairly seriously, as behooved the son of a true dude wrangler. I led people riding nearly every day, and did a certain amount of horse catching, saddling, and unsaddling. I participated in whatever group activities were being promoted, impromptu baseball games or broom polo, both of which I hated. During afterdinner periods, convivial sessions around the fire, the piano, or the card tables were supposed to be enlivened by us wranglers, and if there were any parties or expeditions, unescorted dude girls were to be escorted by us. At one time I was even mistakenly cast as fishing guide. Since I didn't care for fishing and wasn't much good at it, I had to bluff my way through as well as I could. Personally, it was as big a wrench for me from my secluded life up Pacific Creek as the move from the Bar BC had been. I was a pretty backward twenty-four-year-old in many ways, introverted and shy, spoiled by my dream world up country, timid with strangers, especially those of my own generation. On the other hand, though often perplexed and scared, I was earnest and comparatively reliable and experienced.

The most perplexing and perhaps even intimidating, if also exhilarating, aspect of this life had nothing to do with the so-called job. This was the sex-and-Jackson-nightlife that flourished about me among my fellow dude wranglers and the girls on the ranch. For there was no doubt that we were the Fast Set, and we intended to keep up our somewhat spurious reputation. Not really very much happened, in fact; but we looked and acted "fast," and the older dudes were encouragingly shocked, and we were rather proud of our reputations.

The core group included Frank Galey, heir apparent of the White Grass, whose mother, now a widow once more as Mrs. Hammond, owned and ran the ranch with Frank's help. Then there were my other two co-wranglers, Jack White (just graduated from West Point) and Badger (whose real name I can't remember). These were the males. The females consisted basically of Susie Page and Olga Morgan, from Philadelphia. Susie was a cabin girl and worked a good deal harder than we did. Olga was there as a dude with her family. Other girls came and went and also some other boys. Badger was on the ranch especially as the pursuer of Susie. Jack snagged Olga as partner. Frank had many outside female interests, mostly down in Jackson, that we never really knew. Towards the end of the summer a sassy girl named Marty Lou Connor arrived and tried to pin Frank down. Also late in the season I met Dorothy Flagg, the Philadelphia niece of Jeanne de Rham; so all of us ended up more or less paired off. As far as I know there was little or none of the modern casual sex going on, at least on the White Grass itself. But there was certainly a lot of 1930-ish necking and a lot of rather conspicuous lolling about in intertwined groups on porch and sofa. This, and our frequent and extremely late sessions in Jackson, gave us our wild reputation. It was fun.

I suppose we looked the part too. Nobody could have been prettier than Susie and Olga. Frank was a model of the big blond charmer, and the rest of us were young and presentable. It must have been a bit like those old Bar BC days when Jean Burt and Polly Newlin fought over Tucker and Reggie and Francis Biddle and Adolph Borie. But our group was totally without literary or esthetic pretensions. Badger played a mean jazz piano and was constantly put to use of an evening. I played accompaniments for Western songs and such, but nobody played the guitar or wrote poems about "Red, ruinous roses."

All of us are grandparents now, or close to it; but only one marriage resulted, the rather surprising one of Susie and Jack White, who were *not* paired off during that summer. I suppose we are all inclined to look back on that time as part of our glimmering, if not necessarily flaming, youth. Healthy, handsome, comparatively irresponsible, out West, unattached, old enough but not too old—it's a special period in life that certainly never gets repeated and that makes up the "Old West" for many people who have just that sort of experience.

Susie Page was a cousin of mine, a bit like Elena de Struve in character as a somewhat carelessly gotten up animal lover. Unlike Elena she was slim and athletic and with a special pert, dégagé exuberance and casualness that seemed more provocative than it actually was meant to be. Her attitudes were more an expression of not caring very much whether boys liked her or not. But they did. She was dark and tousled haired and big eyed. Olga was fair and demure. They complemented each other nicely.

Badger was terribly in love with Susie, and insanely jealous. He was always plaguing me, as Susie's cousin, with inquisitions about her probable feelings towards him. I kept telling him she probably didn't really give him that much thought. He was in agony. He was what I suppose would have been called "cute looking," engaging, gangling, snub-nosed. Susie accepted his devotion in an offhand way, but spent much of her time tagging after various stalwart mountain climbers, bearded and unbearded.

Mountain climbers were the first younger American men to wear beards in the twentieth century, as opposed to the various Old Man So-and-Sos. Badger snarled and sang, "The mountaineers have shaggy ears and great big yellow britches. They slide down dells with hoots and yells, the silly sons of bitches," but it didn't get him anywhere. One of the mountaineers took Susie up Mount Moran. On top she sat straddling a knife edge, with thousand-foot precipices on either side. Her Levis slit open up the back. After they got back down they decided to get married, but they couldn't find a justice of the peace at that time of the evening. As already observed, she didn't marry either a mountaineer or Badger.

Jack White, whom she did marry, was my roommate in an old, dark, crumbling, log bunkhouse near a rushing stream where we did whatever washing we had to. As a roommate he had one drawback, which was that he not only talked but laughed in his sleep. A hollow sepulchral "HA HA HA" would wake me at three in the morning with a nasty chill. Wonder if he ever woke Susie that way? As a future military man he expressed himself by being just as slovenly, messy, unkempt and slouchy as possible. He was a good horseman and delightful companion, full of offbeat and deadpan humors. Whereas Badger and Susie made a rather conspicuous and stormy couple, Olga and Jack were discreet and orderly.

Frank and Marty Lou Connor did not marry nor did I and Dorothy Flagg. She was really too young to be involved with us, and her parents, if they had known, and her aunt, if she'd noticed, might have disapproved. She was not only too young for me, but far too fashionable. Even out West and at seventeen she sported long red fingernails, dangling hair, and cutoff blue jeans, ahead of fashion. Later on she had debut after debut, to which some of our group went. The one in Philadelphia had a great marquee with a goldfish fountain in it. I went with Susie, and as we came in all dressed up, Susie squatted down in front of four hundred giddy guests and started to play with the gold fish. That was Susie. Dorothy's debut in New York took up the Vienese Roof of the Saint Regis. I remember a letter she wrote me on a trip abroad. The stationery was engraved "Dorothy Flagg en route to Europe." Actually Marty Lou Connor would probably have been more my style if she had had any interests outside of Frank. Her father, for instance, was a dude rancher like mine. He was the first and best-known dude and cattle rancher in Florida, based on real cattle cared for by real Western cowboys. Marty was also literary and wrote things that she showed me. But we definitely did not pair off.

As for those evenings in Jackson that took up what seems in retrospect an inordinate amount of our energy, they were spent milling around in bars, gambling, drinking, necking in parked cars, and dancing to cowboy trios until things finally shut down as the sun came up. The best and favorite hangout was the Log Cabin Bar situated on the southwest corner of the square in Jackson and run by Lou Gill. Gill was a friend of my father, on the right side of public affairs, a very taciturn, cynical, homely, pale man who wore a small-brimmed white rancher hat and kept his mouth shut. Almost next door was the Blue Bird Cafe, owned and run by his "fiancée," Miss Kay. As I remember, she was big and bouncy and as talkative as he was

149

silent. The Blue Bird had taken over from Ma Reed's as the place the elite met to eat—the place where Jeanne de Rham held her champagne supper with all the postrodeo bachelors.

Back of the Log Cabin's bar, which was manned by a big, handsome, smiling, dark friend-of-everyone's but sternly watchful man named Steve, was the dancing and gambling area. Gambling was illegal in Wyoming, but flourished during this period. Since the Log Cabin was still owned and operated by local people, the gambling was honest enough and everybody —man, woman, and child—played roulette, craps, blackjack, and poker. If people came to grief, lost everything, and committed suicide as at Monte Carlo, I never heard of it. I favored roulette.

Once and once only I had one of those lucky streaks that make addictive gamblers out of people. I can see why. I started with one chip which cost me a dime (you can see on what a large scale we gambled). I parlayed it up to eight dollars, without one setback: astronomical percentages. I could not lose. I knew I could not lose. I knew beforehand by an especially given ESP just which numbers and colors were going to come up next, as though by divine, or rather demonic, revelation. It was as intoxicating in a very different but almost equally mystical way as my elk-studded ride of 1931. Voices. But perhaps fortunately they never spoke to me again. I did not become a gambler.

Dancing took place at the Log Cabin or at the Jackson dance hall, where we either stomped around in our cowboy boots to "Dark Town Strutters Ball" or clung to each other in dim lighting to "Moonlight on the Colorado." The leading band of the time was that of the before-mentioned Glen Exum, later on famous as a mountain climber along with Paul Petzoldt and others of Susie's mountaineer group. Glen had a spectacularly handsome younger brother with whom Susie was much smitten and of whom Badger was wildly jealous. He was well on his way to becoming a movie star when, a short time later, he suddenly died.

Tourists were only a fringe nuisance then, nearly everyone was either a friend or identifiable. The evenings were always enlivened by fights, such as those put on by the Emery brothers. In between we had long conversations over long drinks embellished with long stories about old days in Jackson; or there were deep dialogues in dark corners with girls about Life. Marty Lou was excellent on the subject of Life. The Reeds would appear in full regalia from the Three Rivers, glamorous in their gold-embroidered Mexican outfits, Katharine slapping down silver dollars on the bar to treat the boys. Alan, as the evening wore on, would become more and more anxious to knife somebody. Usually my sister had to take charge of him and get him home.

We "White Grassers" were dependent on Frank Galey for transportation, and many horrid moments were spent speeding along the one-car road back to the ranch in the earliest hours, going about sixty or seventy. Luckily the road was empty except for a stray moose or two. One night when I couldn't stand hanging around any longer waiting for Frank to leave, I decided to walk home, boots or no boots. I started out at dawn and went up the slope from the valley of the Elk Refuge north of town towards the flats and the Tetons, just as day began to break. The moon was setting in the west, there were northern lights straight ahead of me. In that spectacular rosy display I got halfway to Blacktail Butte, a good five or six miles up the road, before Frank finally came along. I remember that daybreak a good deal more clearly than I do most of my nights in Jackson.

There were, of course, hundreds of other characters in this

summer production starring our Fast Set—Aunt Marion Galey Hammond, for instance, with her mixture of lovable good nature and irrational emotionalism. She drove Frank crazy. There were the Humphrey girls, blondes all charming in totally different ways, dominated by a firm mother who was going to see that they got properly married—and that meant not to one of us.

Most beautiful and dashing was Caroline, an exceptional horsewoman who pulled back her honey-colored hair in a severely becoming fashion and wore swaggering black Western riding clothes and a general look of "I can do anything better than you; what are you going to do about it?" An admirer gave Caroline a handsome, skittish horse. She was determined to master the horse, but it was too much for her. She was thrown, broke her collarbone, had to go to the hospital, and completely lost her nerve. She could barely look at a horse, and I remember the pathetic sight of that fearless horsewoman being led trembling and white faced down the road on an old plug.

This plunge on my part into a real world of sorts, at least an extroverted one, was exciting but sometimes rather excruciating. I was ill at ease one way or another a good deal of the time. I was scared riding strange horses all the time and playing that damned broom polo with a horse that was head shy and reared every time the damned broom swung up in front of his damned face. I was embarrassed by the embarrassment of dudes who couldn't make up their minds whether I was dude or native, embarrassment that reached a low point when a nice woman I had often taken riding tried to tip me on departure and, like a fool, I refused. Another low point was marked when, just to prove I could do it, I signed up to ride a steer in one of the small rodeos at Wilson. I was in a cold sweat for a week before. Then the great moment arrived. I got aboard, I left the chute, the earth came up and smacked me in the ear, and that was that. My was I relieved!

There were of course so many other incidents and people — the smart-aleck Smith girl who got "lost" for a night or two at the end of a pack trip up Death Canyon with one of the horse wranglers. The wrangler's wife did not understand. The Smith girl's very German boyfriend arrived to preen himself on the diving board of our somewhat cracked concrete swimming pool and tell everyone dogmatically but incorrectly just what the altitude of the Grand Teton was. He played the guitar neatly and of course admired music. German music. "Vat I like iss a gut Fu-ga," I can hear him saying around a campfire. He boasted of being a Nazi.

I saw little of the Three Rivers, though I must have visited. It was my last summer in the Hole before World War II. It was the last of my particular Old West, still full of acquaintances from the Bar BC whom I saw at the Log Cabin, still full of my father's friends and their battles over the park, still a place where electricity broke down and roads were bad and closed with snow during the winter — a place where roughnecks and dudes both could afford to scorn and avoid tourists, even in Jackson. I guess the Jackson of that transition period was tawdry and seedy in many ways. The drunkenness praised and practiced by Donald Hough, the slapdash ethics, the corruption of true frontier by creeping civilization were probably unattractive. Our Fast Set was show-off and silly and certainly obnoxious to some of the elders. But to me, and I suspect all who were young with me then, it was what the thirties liked to call "glamorous." Glamorous was a big word then.

It was in any case the last of my personal Old West. Everyone's Old West is inevitably dead and gone, as it was to Owen Wister by 1902. I suspect this will be just as true of twenty year olds of the 1980s as it was as of the 1930s. In that particular way the Old West is always dying, but never dies.

PART THREE: Modern Times, 1950–1970

7.

AFTER THE WAR

AS for World War II, Jackson Hole was hardly the front line. Yet the war affected it as it did everything else in the world. When people say the Hole has changed since, all one has to do is say, "Look at China." Most Jackson Holers of military age served, and that of course helped to broaden their horizons and make the postwar valley a lot less parochial than it had been. There was even a murky and dubious spy story involving the Hole. Van Arsdale, the man who fixed Kohlers, used to tell it.

It involved a nice little German nicknamed Rosie who worked in a Jackson store, kept a set of Goethe over his bed, and was obviously a traveled and educated man. What the German government thought he would find out in Jackson Hole, if indeed he was a spy, it is impossible to imagine. But the Germans are so thorough. Another figure in this vast conspiracy was a handsome skier called Hans of whom Katharine Reed was fond, and who often visited Three Rivers when I wasn't there. He was picked up and Rosie disappeared and they never came back to the valley. Whether the spy ring was fact or fiction, I do not know.

That was as close to war as the Hole itself got, except for the exploits of native sons. The Hole that those sons came back to after 1945 wasn't much changed; but it began to change almost immediately. The tourist business had been in eclipse and the worst sufferers were the dude ranches. All of them closed at least partially and some of them never re-opened. The Bar BC was one of these victims. It had been going downhill steadily since my father left it. The war more or less finished it off, and a series of postwar disasters completed the process. After Irv himself died, a nice young couple called Lyman tried to revive it; but Lyman was drowned crossing the Snake River and his wife died in winter of peritonitis, too far from medical help. Cabins collapsed or burned down, ditches weren't kept up, and though Irv's widow made valiant attempts, as a true dude ranch the Bar BC ceased to exist.

The Three Rivers was also hard hit in its own way. The Browns and the Reeds having fought and left, Halsey Malone having died and the Amorys having quit, only Katharine Merritt was left as a long-term Associate, and she was too busy with medical war work to be able to come out again until the 1950s. My father, who became 60 in 1942, and Frank Giles, who was even older, kept the ranch going by themselves, by hand, doing their best just to prevent things from physically disintegrating.

When the war ended and my brother-in-law, George Atteberry, and I returned from service, all sorts of grandiose dreams for cattle ranches and boys' camps bloomed and died. In the summer of 1946 my father decided to try running the Three Rivers as a regular old-fashioned dude operation, a sort of last hurrah. He got together the families of half a dozen dear old friends and we had crowded, noisy meals at the main cabin, group rides, corral books, picnics, evenings by the fireside, the works. But his heart wasn't really in it anymore.

George and I hated it, as did our wives. They had to act as cabin girls, making beds and cleaning toilets. George was sort of handyman and chauffeur; I was sort of head wrangler. We had a real hired wrangler, a charming but neurotic cowboy called Phil. He was a good wrangler when in condition; but he had an obsession for bronc riding. Every weekend he would go down to Wilson or Jackson, screw up his courage by getting drunk, then ride and be thrown and painfully injured. The rest of the week he spent recovering. I ended up having to do most of his work. I had already had enough of this sort of thing at the White Grass and my experiences in the summer of 1946 finished me as a dude wrangler, along with any ideas of ever trying to run the Three Rivers as a paying proposition.

I was the one who took people out for rides. Some of this was fun, some was not. One family had a stalwart two-hundred-pound teenage son who was pathologically afraid of horses. His father thought it would be good therapy to make him ride, so every morning we gathered at the corral. Father gave a military command. Son mounted trembling to the saddle, his hands in a death grip on the saddle horn. Out we crept, the boy still in a state of shock and flanked by his parents. One time on the trail his mother cried, "Stop, stop!" I stopped. It seemed the boy's enormous foot had come out of the stirrup, and I had to dismount and put it back in for him. On their last ride I took them by accident through a bees' nest. The boy's horse reared and carried on, right at the edge of a steep bank, but he stayed on and did very well indeed. It was the parents who were terrified. I am sure they believe to this day that I did it on purpose (well, not really!).

All these guests, these pals of my parents, were individually charming and collectively scintillating; but, as Frank Giles remarked, it was all chiefs and no Indians. That many commanding personalities gathered closely together created situations. One of the guests, a famously handsome Southern gentleman and fine horseman, enjoyed getting himself up in full Western regalia, chaps and all. He looked just the way the Virginian should have looked. He got a boil on his behind. He not only could not ride, he could not sit comfortably at the table. Nobody was less able to bear this particular kind of humiliation and frustration.

We had as waitress one of the most beautiful little girls I have ever seen. She wasn't more than sixteen, an heiress to a great fortune, and in love with the West. She was also unfortunately in love with the handsome, artistic, and precociously well-developed fifteen-year-old son of one of our dudes. His mother went down to our local post office, Moran, then at the foot of the Jackson Lake dam, to make train reservations home. In those days you went by train, of course, and got your tickets through the Western Union office in Moran. "I've already got two reservations for you, ma'am," said the operator. "A girl came down and made them yesterday." Since the mother had just decided that morning when she was going to leave, she was surprised. She was even more surprised when she discovered that our waitress was planning to elope with her son at his mother's expense.

Our next waitress was a college girl of high educational attainments but weak will who was enslaved by a wandering, cross-eyed, pseudocowboy of dubious origin. She had first been a waitress at the White Grass, but they fired her because she insisted that they hire the boyfriend too. She accepted our offer on the same conditions. She was marvelous as a waitress and could discuss Goethe and Proust at any time of the day.

Boyfriend was helpless at everything. He couldn't chop wood without breaking the axe. He couldn't ride a horse without giving it saddle sores. He lamed my father's prize horse, riding at a gallop without permission. He couldn't even make hay.

In those happy days before motorized balers, loose hay was pitched by hand onto wagons to be taken to the barn for stacking. Our lone cowboy stood on top of the hayload declaiming his own poetry, pitchfork in hand, but not doing any pitching. He couldn't write poetry either.

When my father discovered that this second waitress was also planning to elope, he telegraphed her father. Father flew out, somehow hired a helicopter, landed right on the Three Rivers, snatched up his daughter, and flew away. We immediately fired the boyfriend and did without waitresses for the rest of the summer.

The climax of our, or at least my, trouble occurred towards the end of the season when the grown-up dudes on a trip to Jackson fell in with Old Man So-and-So at one of the bars. He was a famous if not veracious teller of tall tales, and they were all so struck by his talents that they arranged for him to come up to the ranch, lead all the adolescents out to a camp and campfire up the creek, cook them lunch, and tell them tales.

Old Man So-and-So of course promised and of course, after his usual full evening, forgot. We had a horse all packed up with gear, and the kids' horses saddled and waiting. When the old man didn't show up, we (that is, Dad, Frank, and I) suggested that we call the trip off or at least change it to a manageable sandwich picnic. Nothing doing. The show must go on. None of us had the time or inclination to take a pack outfit on such a jaunt. The parents countered with the proposition that we just turn the kids loose with the pack outfit, let them unpack it, and leave it up on the creek to be picked up later. When I turned that proposition down, one of the more commanding fathers disdainfully pulled out his checkbook, which for some odd reason he happened to have right on him (I guess he never moved without it), and offered to pay for the gear. At which time I told him to go to hell in those words and realized once and for all that I would never make the dude wrangler my father had been. Frank was haying, my father was tied up, I involved in something; still and all, true dude wranglers would have managed somehow without offending even such officious dudes. It was sort of a test case.

Most of our dudes, I believe, enjoyed most of their time, but we had all been wrecks by the time fall came. We hadn't made enough money to justify the wear and tear, so after another period of discussion and argument, we all decided we would have to rebuild the Association on the old plan; but this time from scratch without a group of Bar BC dudes to start with.

Katharine Merritt remained faithful and was once more able to come West. We reconstructed our partnership with a new set of friends. Adrian Malone was eventually solvent enough as a San Francisco architect to take over his father's cabin. Two other new partners, the Sherrerds and the Untermyer family, took over the Reed and Amory cabins respectively. My wife and I lived in the old Bispham-Brown cabin. For quite a few years it was not unlike the Good Old Days.

Frank Giles retired soon after that fatal dude summer. Emma had died, Lamar had moved to the Coast, and Frank had married a sweetly selfish Utah widow named Annie. Frank and Annie ate with us at the main cabin and she exercised her gifts for being gently exasperating.

After Frank left, my father had the idea of farming out the foremanship of the ranch to anyone who felt he could combine minimal foreman duties with an attempt to make a private living off the place. As a result, a series of picturesque and charming Westerners filed through the Three Rivers, each contributing his bit to the ranch's gradual disintegration. The Carlows were as delightful and well-mannered a couple as could be met with, he an expert carpenter, she an expert bridge player. They looked on the place as a sort of retirement home. The Mangum family who succeeded them stemmed from Virgin, Utah, which is nearby to Hurricane. They had family connections in the Hole and were prolific, handsome, quarrelsome, and inefficient. There was a patriarch with a grizzled mustache who was the nominal foreman; but work was actually done by various good-looking sons or nephews. There was Carlos and there was Carlisle. Carlos, a sweet-natured and cherubic-faced muscular giant, gentle as a lamb during the week, made his reputation down country during the weekend as a no-holds-barred brawler who had to be continually rescued from jail, lachrymose and repentant. Equally gentle but less hefty blond Carlisle, surely one of the nicest men ever born, would look upon some piece of botched ranch work and say philosophically, "What you caint do with your haid you gotta do with your back."

The Mangums had innumerable children, some retarded, some angelic. Most angelic was a four year old named Ronny (pronounced Rawny). I remember Rawny sitting on the floor of my parents' cabin looking at an old school primer. In it was a silly picture of an unbearably cute little Classic faun, his head flung back playing on panpipes. "Wot's that little girl doin' with that there whiskey?" asked Rawny. The Mangums and their innumerable wives, relatives, sick children, family quarrels, and fetching personalities left to be succeeded by Ted Adams.

Ted Adams came closest to making a success of the venture, since he was able to use the ranch as a basis for fall hunting expeditions. He was an ideal cowboy in looks—lean, blond, dashing, and of course full of charm as all our temporary pseudoforemen were. He had an even more charming wife nicknamed Nubs. The basic trouble was the arrangement itself. In order to make any sort of living at horse raising and fall hunting, Ted neglected the ranch maintenance and dude wrangling, neither of which he was very good at in any case. By this time my father was dying, though still very much in charge, and was not easy to work for.

In 1946 during the ill-fated dude summer my father had been still at the top of his powers. He published two of his most successful books in the forties, his history of Philadelphia called *Holy Experiment* (1945) and his Philadelphia novel, *Along These Streets* (1942). He was still in good health. But from then on he steadily declined. He was troubled with asthma and weakened by a series of strokes. He couldn't write any more, Scribner's took all his books out of print, he suffered from bouts of melancholia and irrational fears that he was going bankrupt. He grew weaker and weaker and finally during the summer of 1954, right after his fiftieth reunion at Princeton he died in the Jackson hospital and was buried above town in the Jackson graveyard.

When he died, the Adamses quit. I for one was sorry to see them go, though the ranch was certainly in poor physical shape by the time they left. Since my father was the core about which the whole organization of the Three Rivers had been built, he left a vacuum that never could be filled. He really loved to be surrounded by people, he attracted them and hypnotized them and it was his personality that really held the Association of the ranch together. The Adamses had been kind to my father in his last days, and he was the only one on the ranch that really got along with them, though nobody could have been more delightful social companions.

A more stylish-looking all-Western couple than the Adamses in full party regalia you never did see.

An odd but equally glamorous if rather sinister-looking side-burned cowboy named Bob Hayes came to our rescue when the Adamses left. He was temporarily unmarried and brought various cowboy friends up to batch with him. His real avocation was bronc busting, and impromptu shows were put on in our corral. An English girl arrived to visit, and I will never forget her pop-eyed admiration as these stalwart sons of the West mucked up our corral showing off on bucking horses for her benefit. Very little ranch work got done. The foreman's house, once the Giles family center, became a shambles.

Finally and at last and at just about the last possible moment, the Jerald Jacobsons came and stayed till the end in 1979. The ranch was rescued just as it was about to collapse physically and morally. But then also finally and at last, Pedro the cook retired after his some thirty-five years of service. So we began to go through the same series of annual replacements in the kitchen that we had had in the foreman's cabin.

Some of these replacements were equally picturesque and temporary. There were the Yaples, for instance, who quite literally wandered in off the road and stayed for a couple of years. He was a large, florid, patriarchal chef who habitually dressed in white Western costume with a great white sombrero. He spent his free time making meringues or rolls just for fun. He had worked in many odd places, including a high-class hotel-bordello in Las Vegas owned by movie actress Clara Bow and her lover, and had marvelous tales to tell of bad high doings. I got an Eastern editor interested in a Western cookbook that was to be a collaboration between Yaple and myself; but the Yaples wandered out as they had wandered in and the volume of recipes and tales of life in camp and brothel never got written. And we never did get a permanent cook like Pedro.

Then the new Associates, so painfully acquired after World War II, began to leave one by one. Don Sherrerd got a bad back and could not indulge in his expeditions of lake fishing; Adrian Malone settled permanently in Sheridan where he could practice architecture and ride all at once. So it, and they, went. We reached the same point of vacancy as in 1945 — nobody left but the Burts and Katharine Merritt, in her eighties but still going strong.

When, finally, in 1979 the ranch lease was up, there were no active associates left except the two "younger Burts," no longer so young. Our children really were too young and busy to do more than visit; Katharine Merritt had been incapacitated by an accident; the Jacobsons had had enough of fifty-degree-below winters after twenty-five years. There was obviously no sense trying to continue the Three Rivers along the old lines. Attempts to interest the park in preserving the place and having institutions use it for summer seminars failed. Beginning in 1980 the cabins started to be sold and moved off, and one of Wyoming's most beautiful and characteristic spreads, with its special literary associations and architectural charms, dissolved and disappeared. It was a sad loss to Jackson Hole's history and its human, as opposed to purely natural, beauty.

For a good thirty years after 1950, however, the Three Rivers struggled along. The routine of rides and good times was punctuated by the same occasional quarrels and sudden disasters that are as characteristic of the Far West as the thin air and high tempers.

After my father's death, however, things were different. The ranch became more of a plain summer place, much less a headquarters for the valley's conservation battles and Democratic politics. Dick Winger survived of the original group; Harold Fabian, Rockefeller's most active lawyer in the original Snake River Land Company, spent the summers in the Hole; Ken Chorley often visited at the JY. Once in awhile Horace Albright dashed through the Hole as though convoyed by motorcycles. But the battle at last was won. The Hole was saved. The war was over too and Hitler was defeated; Roosevelt was dead. My father's great causes were accomplished.

I think part of the reasons for his collapse in health during those last years was a reaction to the emotional letdown of these victories and the consequent emptiness. Later politics and conservation battles were more confused and less interesting to him.

On the Three Rivers ranch life went on. A whole new generation of children, including mine and the Jacobson's, grew up, became adolescent, left the nest. My mother continued to write into her eighties. I wrote at the Three Rivers now too. My mother rode regularly until she was eighty-two. Katharine Merritt went on a pack trip when she was eighty-seven. Great causes and battles and local animosities played no role in this private postwar world. The history of Wyoming was not much affected by anything emanating from Pacific Creek Valley from 1950 on.

Meanwhile, outside of our hideaway the New Jackson Hole was evolving. The old Jackson Hole had been based on horses and cattle and horseback-riding dudes. Everything—cabins, furniture, saddles, clothes—was indigenously Western and all of us wanted to keep it that way. Cattle was primary; tourism secondary. We still felt part of the Frontier.

By 1950 all that had changed. Whereas in the past the contrast had been between Tenderfeet and Roughnecks, it was now between Natives and Tourists. Nobody much had used that Eastern summer-resort word "native" to describe Jackson Holers in the old days. The tourists were a despised group excluded by dude ranches and catered to offhandedly and condescendingly by bars, cabin courts, and shops in Jackson only.

Tourism is king now; dude ranching and cattle ranching are secondary. Two new avocations, the world afoot of mountain climbing and hiking in the summer, and skiing in the winter, have ousted riding as favorite local sports and skills. No old-time Westerner would have dreamed of walking when he could ride, except in the processes of fishing and hunting. Mountain climbing is more respectable for Westerners than hiking; but most of the important mountain climbers in the Hole, from the days of Susie and her shaggy lovers on, have been from outside. Another brand-new spectacle has been boat life on Jackson Lake. A few freaks used to have motor boats. The Woodwards showed how queer they were by canoeing on Leigh Lake. Anybody fool enough to attempt to go down the Snake in a boat deserved to be drowned, and some people were. After the war all this had changed. There were even sailboats on Jackson Lake, not to mention hundreds of powerboats and waterskiers. Rubber rafts bob down the Snake every day by the dozens.

Of all these new sports, skiing is most native and has had the most impact. Jackson Holers always skied cross-country in winter. The people who spent those early winters on the Bar BC skied down the benches with hoots and yells like those same mountaineers with shaggy ears. They were pretty amateur about it. The first serious downhill skiing began after the war on the slopes of Snow King Mountain above Jackson, right next to the graveyard where my father is buried. Local boys and girls became not only Wyoming but national and international champions. It was a bit like the fame of the Tetons themselves. Sitting in a restaurant in Lausanne, Switzerland, in winter, we were idly glancing at the television, turned as usual to Swiss championship ski races. Suddenly and conspicuously Karen Budge, kin of Jim Budge of the early Bar BC days, flashed by with French commentary on the screen. In an exuberance more Wyoming than Vaudois, I exclaimed to the waitress that this was a girl from *"mon pays."* How is it possible to express her polite Swiss lack of interest?

So a big new development called Teton Village has been built at the foot of the mountains right below the park boundaries and above Wilson. It is all fake Swiss architecture and half-genuine Swiss restaurants dominated by genuine Swiss maîtres d'hôtel, still full of polite Swiss lack of interest in anything human. I can't help wishing that some night a bunch of the boys would break in drunk and shoot up the place, disturbing the guests in their blazers and high-necked sweaters and snappy pantsuits and long dresses, perhaps even causing the headwaiter to raise his eyebrows. Rich people have built beautiful modern houses among the aspens and mosquitoes, houses that look as though they had been flown in by helicopter from a Denver suburb. The inhabitants play golf and tennis all day and then go to those Swiss restaurants at night.

After dinner, flushed with wine (not whiskey), the diners in the restaurants can go on to superb concerts at Teton Village almost any night in July and August and hear almost anything from full orchestra to chamber music in a brand-new acoustically splendid concert hall. For Culture has come with a rush too, and Jackson Hole has one of the best summer music festivals in the country.

So what with native kids on Swiss television and Swiss res-
taur+anteurs at Teton Village and skiers arriving in the Hole
by plane in midwinter and snowmobiles dashing all over the
snow and powerboats dashing all over the lake and people
playing tennis and even squash and building big houses and
condominiums and most of the people never even seeing a
horse all year, except perhaps at a rodeo, the Old Hole sure
as hell has changed.

The music is wonderful, many of the new people are great
(even if they do play golf), and the modern houses are really
beautiful, for Jackson has made the leap straight from the log
cabin to Frank Lloyd Wright and beyond with no break or
transition. Painters flourish, and every other store in Jackson
is an art gallery of some kind. I wish I really liked it all. I enjoy
it, but that is not the same as liking, much less approving, of
the New Jackson Hole and the New West of which it is a vital
and representative part.

The New West, centered in boom cities like Denver and
Phoenix, certainly has much to recommend it. It is enthusiastic,
youthful, healthy, sporting, and deeply involved in art and
ecology and Western history. It is not frontier backwater but
forefront America. The New West is now being settled largely
by people, often from other places, who live in it because they
want to, not because they have to. Above all, it is forming and
acquiring a regional independence, even economically, quite
different from the mere passing phase of frontier, which is
bound to dissolve—whatever its charms and virtues—as a second generation (of which I am one) grows up and the country
settles down.

But, as far as I can see, New Westerners do not sit around
campfires telling half-hour masterpieces of comic art. Do they
hear Voices in the wilderness above the bugling of elk? On the

whole the New West reminds me of the Reeds, all dressed up in their war paint and rarin' to go (to hell, sometimes) than it does of the kind of West the Burts, senior and junior, have known and loved.

There is, fortunately—as part of the culture of the New West—a great upsurge in interest in wildlife and natural science and ecology and the balances of the earth, which is certainly an advance on the often crudely exploitive attitudes of much of the Old West. Few Western elective politicians nowadays would dare be so blatantly in favor of Progress, or as opposed to Conservation, as the older Wyoming politicians habitually were. This is one area in which the gain seems to be generally positive. Exploitation is as much of a threat as ever, maybe even greater, but the voices raised against it are loud, forceful, many, effective, and above all native, not just the happy few of my father's day. This is one of the brighter sides of life in the New West.

Mount Hayden and Mount Moran, by Thomas Moran. Tetons from the rear, 1876. Note identification of the Grand Teton as "Mount Hayden." Courtesy of Ridell Photos, Jackson, Wyo.

Jackson Lake, by William Henry Jackson, 1879. Note effect of forest fire. Courtesy of Ridell Photos.

Still from Katharine Burt movie *Snow Blind*, about 1921.

Katharine Burt in Hollywood, 1919. Standing (from left): Le Roy
Stuart, Gouverneur Morris, Sam Goldwyn, Rupert Hughes. Sitting
(from left): Gertrude Atherton, Katharine Burt, Mary Roberts Rinehart, Rita Wyman.

Fade-out of Bar BC home movie, starring Gracie Lewis and Bill Howard.
Off for the honeymoon!

Wallace Beery and friends, with Struthers Burt hunched up in back row.

Mrs. Nathaniel ("Winkie") Burt and favorite horse,
Ginger.

Nathaniel Burt on the fence.

Margery Burt (right) and Atteberry nieces, about 1952.

Chris Burt and Julie Jacobson, about 1957.

Jerry Jacobson on Lucky, front of Reed cabin.

Katharine Burt's last ride on Ginger, with Nathaniel Burt. Front of Reed cabin, about 1966.

8.

CULTURE AND FAREWELL

ONE of the more pleasant characteristics of the New West is its interest in the arts, particularly painting. There is in fact a boom in work by painters of the West. A Denver collector, for instance, recently bought a Thomas Moran for over half a million dollars. But Jackson Hole itself has always had its curious connections with the arts, and this has been true of the West in general, in a special sort of way.

The cowboy West, as myth and symbol, was created by men of talents like Frederic Remington and Owen Wister, and their traditions keep going. Every Western bar and motel office is crowded with hand-painted oil paintings, every Westerner has a feeling for Charley Russell and Will James. Indians, north and south, have produced their own truly indigenous interpretations of the country's color and spirit, and this too has been absorbed and appreciated. Altogether there is and has been lots of art in the West, though not always lots of good art.

The connections between the Hole and art begin right at the beginnings of its modern, as opposed to its earliest, history. Two peaks of the Teton range are named for creative artists — Mount Moran, north of the Grand Teton, and Mount Wister, south of it. Both the painter and writer have early connections with the valley, though Moran never actually seems to have set foot in it. Wister did, and it is the art of writing that is most closely associated with Jackson Hole.

The visual artists came first, however. Thomas Moran, who is so prominently memorialized by his mountain, was the first artist to paint the Tetons. He was born in England in 1837, the son of humble parents who were weavers. The family emigrated in 1844 and settled in the textile center of Kensington, a northern borough of Philadelphia. Thomas Moran was merely the most prominent of a whole family circle of artists only a trifle less numerous than the Peales. Three brothers were successful painters, Thomas (landscapes), Edward (seascapes), and Peter (animals). Beside this there were wives, sisters, in-laws, children who were involved in the visual arts in some way—at least a dozen in all.

Thomas was by far the most famous of them. He painted in the East and the Middle West until the 1870s. His first Western pictures were illustrations for articles about Yellowstone that appeared in *Scribner's* magazine in 1871. Moran had never been West and did all his work from crude sketches by others. He used his imagination to flesh out these illustrations and the results were naturally more fanciful than faithful. But on the strength of this work he was allowed to accompany the second expedition of Ferdinand Hayden later in 1871. This was the first important scientific exploration of the wonders of Yellowstone. Moran had never been on a horse before, and was a rather fragile explorer. He had to tie a pillow on the saddle to ease his bony bottom. But he was such a good sport and engaging companion and so enthusiastic about the country that he became a favorite with the whole group of outfitters and scientists.

His best friend on this trip was the pioneer photographer William Henry Jackson. Jackson, a native of upper New York state (born 1843), had left home, already a professional photographer, because of a disappointment in love. He was a seasoned Westerner by the time of the Hayden expedition. He had earned his living driving an ox team across the continent towards California and driving horses back, and he had been a member of a previous Hayden expedition the year before. He and Moran got on famously, and between them they recorded the beauties and oddities of Yellowstone in paint and photograph so effectively that the region immediately became famous. Along with the expedition's scientific data, the Moran-Jackson pictures served as a basis for the establishment of Yellowstone as the first national park in 1872.

An expedition that same year of 1872 reexplored the Yellowstone, and a special, smaller, splinter group was sent down to look over the Tetons. Moran couldn't accompany this Teton group, but his friends who explored the mountains and the Hole made him an "honorary member" in absentia. While they were happily naming all the peaks of the Tetons for their friends — they dubbed the Grand Teton Mount Hayden — they called one of the most impressive of the mountains Mount Moran.

Moran himself didn't see the Tetons until 1879, and then from the Idaho side. He did, however, paint the first, and still among the best, pictures of the peaks, but all from the backside, so to speak. He never saw, much less painted, the world-famous view of Mount Moran from the east reflected in Jackson Lake.

Jackson also made the first photographs of the Tetons and also from the Idaho side. This was in 1872; but he did get into the Hole in 1879, made some pictures, and mentions the valley in his autobiography. He says little about it, except that he thought the name "Hole" distressing.

Jackson Lake is not named for the photographer, but for that obscure trapper David Jackson, who gave his name to the entire valley. It *should,* however, have been named for the photographer, and what is to prevent us nowadays from thinking of it as his memorial? Why doesn't the park officially rededicate it to William Henry, who is far more famous now than shadowy David? Moran and Jackson certainly ought to be visually associated in that grand junction of peak and water.

Both men went on to long and successful later careers. Moran died in 1926, aged eighty-nine. Jackson died in 1942, aged ninety-eight. Both were active to the end. They had many important later rewards and adventures, but never worked in the Yellowstone-Teton area again. Yet these early pictures remain their most famous productions.

Since then, probably more paintings have been blobbed and more photographs clicked of the Tetons than of any other mountains in America. By now Jackson Hole has many resident painters, some of them making a good living out of this visual gold mine. It would be invidious to single out a few. Yet despite the excellence of modern masters, no one, as far as I am concerned, has quite come up to Moran, especially his watercolors, in catching the exact color and quality of the landscape. Certainly none has achieved his national reputation, once great, then dim, now reemergent. Among photographers, famous Ansel Adams has carried on the tradition begun by famous William Henry Jackson. The competition here has been enormous, for no peaks in the world are more photogenic and more photographed.

The Burts, senior or junior, have had almost no personal contact with any of the resident Jackson Hole painters, past or present. The then and once again famous New England artist Frank Benson (known for his game birds) was at the ranch in 1917; but perhaps the closest contact was N. C. Wyeth, who did a splendid illustration for one of my father's earlier books of short stories. The picture, illustrating a story called "Devilled Sweetbreads," has a cook chasing a fugitive across the foreground with a knife. In the background is the Bar BC version of the Grand Teton, beautifully done; but Wyeth never saw it. In fact, he claimed to have made the scene up, but he must have had a photograph. Maxfield Parrish, another illustrator who might have done justice to the mountains, never saw them either, as far as I know.

Literature has had a more continuous and intimate connection with the valley, but one that begins later. Discounting scientific and historic reports, the first writing to bring the Tetons to popular notice was Owen Wister's *The Virginian*. Though of course most of the novel is not laid in the Hole, the hero's friend Shorty does get shot and buried right in the Tetons. Some have thought the final romantic honeymoon on a river island really depicts the Hole, but it is specifically indicated as being along the Wind River.

Wister came to Jackson Hole in his first years in the West, not on his original trip in 1885, but later on hunting expeditions during summers from 1887 through 1893. He penetrated the valley, camped close to the Three Rivers near the Snake and Buffalo Fork, and has left some pretty vivid pictures of the rough, empty, unexplored valley of that time — ninety years ago, but a good decade or two after the Hayden survey. On one of his trips he insisted on fording the Snake so as to get to lakes at the foot of the Tetons that the maps told him must be there. His guide said there were no such lakes, but by following the sound of rushing water at the base of the mountains, the Wister party got to them, much to his triumph and the chagrin of the guide. This gives some idea of how little was known about the Hole then, though permanent settlement had already begun.

Owen Wister was an unlikely person to create the myth of the cowboy. Born in 1860 in the lap of Old Philadelphia luxury, his early ambition was to be a composer of serious music. At Harvard University he became intimate with Theodore Roosevelt. Forced by his stuffy father to become a lawyer and intimidated intellectually by his bluestocking mother, he had a nervous breakdown in 1885. The "nervous breakdown" had just been more or less invented by the Philadelphia doctor, psychiatrist, and later famous novelist, S. Wier Mitchell, an old family friend. His not very novel cure consisted of simply sending young Owen west for a change of scenery.

His arrival in Wyoming, accurately described at the beginning of *The Virginian*, and his summer based on Major Wolcott's ranch in the Bighorn Basin cured his breakdown and converted him to the wonders of the West, not just its wild scenery but its wild inhabitants, particularly the cowboy. He began writing Western short stories in 1891. The first one, "Hank's Woman," was composed in one night in the library of the Philadelphia Club, the city's, and indeed the nation's, oldest and most rigidly exclusive. The story was published in 1892. After that he used his old law office as a writing room. His stories were almost immediately popular. Much of their popularity was due to the illustrations by Frederic Remington, another Easterner in love with the West.

Wister met him by chance in Yellowstone in 1893. Wister had just come up there from camping along Buffalo Fork. They were close friends for years, and both close friends of Roosevelt. The careers of this trio reached their climax in and around 1900. Roosevelt became president in 1901 and Wister's *The Virginian* was published in 1902. It was then and has been ever since one of the great American best sellers. Oddly enough, it was not illustrated by Remington as it should have been. Roosevelt, however, followed its creation with avid interest and even censored a passage in it because he thought it too brutal. I would suppose this to be the only novel ever edited by a president of the United States. Wister's mother was very superior about it, and compared it to the writings of Ouida. Faint praise could have been no fainter. Henry James rather properly thought the end should have been grandly tragic. Remington wrote his own Western novel, but it was not very successful.

In 1911, after another nervous breakdown similar to the one in 1885, Wister once more came West, this time to Jackson Hole itself with wife and children. He went to the JY where my father was beginning his career as dude wrangler, and Wister was one of the dudes he wrangled. They were much together during that summer. My father—as another lover of the West, another Philadelphian, and another at least would-be writer—had much in common with Wister and was awed, fascinated, and honored by the company of the great man. He has recorded his impression in a preface he wrote to a special fancy illustrated edition of *The Virginian* put out by the Heritage Press in 1951. It is surely the best short portrait and analysis of Wister in print, written with an inside understanding of both Wister's Philadelphia and Wister's West.

In that preface my father tells of the traumatic incident that occurred in the following year, 1912, while the Wisters were again on the JY. Mrs. Wister's father died. His name was also Wister, a cousin. The Owen Wisters, marooned without newspapers, heard about the death belatedly. They hurried back East and discovered that the newspapers had mistaken Owen's father-in-law for Owen himself. There were obituaries and above all literary summations that tended to dismiss him as a first-rate second-rate writer. Unlike Mark Twain who was able to take similar premature burial as a joke — "highly exaggerated" — Wister was devastated.

For a man who had been one of the greatest literary successes in American history, advised by President Roosevelt and Henry James, this was all too much. In any case he wrote nothing more of significance, though he lived until 1938. His good second novel, *Lady Baltimore*, had not been wildly popular and he never wrote another full-length work of fiction. His wife died in 1913, leaving him with six children. He could not bear to come back to his new ranch in the Hole. He would never talk about the West to his children. His Old West had died before 1900. Wister became president of the Philadelphia Club, the city's highest honor, got very excited about the heroism of England during World War I, though of course the Wisters were German, and wrote a satire against Prohibition. Between them, Wister, Remington, and Roosevelt did more than any others to create the cowboy as myth and symbol. Yet nobody ever remained a more quintessential dude than that exmusician and clubman, Owen Wister.

The literary laying on of hands was fairly direct. My father, like Wister, was also a Philadelphian who had escaped to the West and wanted to be a writer. He quite literally sat at Wister's feet, and carried on Wister's tradition, but with a reverse twist since his best-known works were about Philadelphia, not Wyoming. My mother actually wrote more about the West than my father did, and she not only sat but lay at Wister's feet.

In the first year of her coming to Wyoming she took a long and exhausting ride from the Bar BC to the JY. She fell asleep on the way. When she got to her destination, her horse stopped abruptly and she fell off, right in front of Wister. She came to with him towering over her, his head on one side, taking notes in his little pocket notebook on just how a lady looks when thrown from a horse. He always took such careful notes of things that struck him, much to the envy of my father who could never manage to keep a notebook of that kind. It was such detailed jottings on Western phrases, customs, dress, and ways of living that made his fiction, like Remington's pictures, authentic records of Western life, for all their romanticism.

My father was far more of a Westerner than Wister ever was. He really learned to do the things professionally that Wister observed, recorded, or only occasionally practiced. He roped and rode broncs and worked cattle. He guided and packed and even cooked in the hills. But he didn't actually write very much about all of this. He wrote about the Philadelphia that Wister could not get himself to approach fictionally. Wister never went on with the novel he began about what he called "Monopolis."

My father wrote many short stories about the West, but his most famous Western short story, "Water Hole" (included in the first O'Brien collection of 1915), was located in the desert Southwest. The story that first established his literary reputation, "Each in his Generation," and that won the O'Henry Memorial Prize in 1920, dealt with Wister's Philadelphia. His best-known work of Western nonfiction, *Powder River* (1938), describes Wister's plains country in central Wyoming. Only the *Diary of a Dude Wrangler* (1924) really tackles the scene of Jackson Hole. His second novel, *The Delectable Mountains* (1927), has a whole midsection laid in the Hole and pictures the devastation wrought by the Jackson Lake dam. Joe LePage appears there as a fictional character. It has always seemed odd to me that he never wrote a complete novel laid in the valley.

It is his novel about Philadelphia, *Along These Streets* (1942), that is best remembered nowadays. He wrote many articles and newspaper pieces dealing with aspects of Jackson Hole, but little of that is in book form. Some of his poetry also was inspired by the West, but no complete novel.

My mother's career, though far less seriously considered, has been more durable. All my father's books are out of print, but many of hers are still available. She began writing silly stories for English girls' magazines, like that early western, "Tommy Tenderfoot." Then during her first years as housekeeper and mother on the Bar BC, she incubated *The Branding Iron*, which swept the country in 1919. It combined passion and vivid Western background, and was followed by two others of the kind, *Hidden Creek* (1920) and *Snow Blind* (1921). After this she settled down to the almost annual production of books, some of them set against the Tetons, some not. Nearly all were serialized in women's magazines, and they supported the family between the more esoteric and wider-spaced successes of my father. My mother's earliest novels, *The Branding Iron* and its sequels, began appearing again in paperback, as of the seventies and her nineties—a renaissance of Romance and of the first fiction about Jackson Hole written more than sixty years ago.

The book called *Desperate Scenery* by Eliot Paul was not published until 1954, but it too describes the Jackson Hole of those ancient days, specifically the building of that infamous Jackson Lake dam in the winter of 1910-11. Full of Paul's usual collection of quite incredibly lurid characters, it is condescending to the "natives" of the Hole, particularly one real character, Ben Sheffield. He was running his famous hunting lodge right at the lake outlet where the dam was built. As an engineer,

Paul is decidedly pro-dam. Sheffield, whose scenery was desperately ruined, was not so enthusiastic.

The dam was, however, a tremendous engineering feat. The whole concrete and steel structure was built sixty miles from the nearest railroad during one of the valley's worst winters. The gates, manufactured elsewhere, had to be brought in over a specially constructed road, not Teton Pass but a track around the north end of the Tetons now disused. The gates had to arrive before the snow got too deep, and then the concrete to hold them had to be poured in below-freezing weather, surrounded by wooden chambers steam-heated to prevent the damp material from freezing. It was an epic, even if one destructive to the beauty of Jackson Lake. The dam still holds. The resultant devastation of the shores, an unbelievable tangle of dead trees, remained an eyesore until the Civilian Conservation Corps in the thirties, and then the Park Service, gradually cleared it up. The lake is beautiful once more; but the awesome memorial to Thomas Moran and William Henry Jackson has never been quite the same since Eliot Paul and his collection of engineering freaks got through with it.

I suppose I myself have carried on the literary torch lighted by Wister (even to the extent of wanting to be a composer) and kept going by my parents, but in an even more perverse way. Though actually born in Wyoming, I have never published anything about the West except poetry and a juvenile version of my father's *Powder River* called *War Cry of the West*. My best-known book, like my father's, has been a book about Philadelphia—precisely that Philadelphia from which my father and Wister escaped to go West. Since I have never actually lived in Philadelphia, it has had something of the exotic glamour for me that Wyoming had for Wister.

The principal chronicler of a later Jackson Hole, the Jackson

Hole of those raffish gambling and drinking nights of just before World War II and just after, was Donald Hough. He came
to the Hole from the Middle West and the Coast in the late
twenties. He introduced himself to my father and did a funny
caricature of him in 1928 (which still hangs in my writing room
along with a sketch of a cowboy by Frank Benson as of 1917).
He settled in Jackson with a beautiful and long-suffering wife
and a son, and proceeded to drink and write, somewhat in
that order. When sober he was full of ebullience and charm.
When drunk he was surly, lecherous, and belligerent. He pictures with wonderful accuracy the smell, feel, and quality of
the bars and roughnecks and dudes of my Fast Set period, but
with special emphasis on those winters that were still isolated
and still untarnished by skiers and snowmobiles. Two of his
books, *Snow Above Town* (1943) and *Cocktail Hour in Jackson
Hole* (1956), though they gave offense to some, certainly caught
that exact moment of the Hole's transition from Old West to
New West. Rather in the spirit of Eliot Paul, his Jackson seems
overly littered with queer characters and discarded bottles, but
hunting and blizzards and ranch life come into the picture too.
He wrote many other books, stories, and articles, and everybody in the Hole knew him; but eventually drink and disorder
got to be too much for his family and friends. What sounded
amiably boozy in print could be pretty awful in alcoholic real
life. He died in a fire in Jackson, more or less a broken derelict.

Since my father died in 1954 and Donald Hough in 1968,
there has not been any other true free-lance writer-resident in
the Hole with that sort of national reputation. Many writers
have passed through, many have used the Hole as background,
including the Countess in a first novel. There has been a mass
of good writing about its history, human and natural, but no

literary figures as closely identified as my parents and Hough.

My father, as a well-known writer, attracted other well-known writers as visitors; for in those days it would seem any well-known writer knew all the others. As one of Maxwell Perkins's Scribner's protégés, my father had met Ernest Hemingway (he knew F. Scott Fitzgerald earlier, as of Princeton). When Hemingway came through Jackson Hole hunting, it was natural for him to drop in at the Bar BC, as of 1928.

The occasion happened to be my mother's birthday in early September, and she was sick in bed. We children, in our teens, were entertaining her with a play we had written. It was a spoof on the drearier sort of 1920 epic called "Water Water O God," which ended by everyone being swept away by a flood. To symbolize this watery denoument, we opened the door to throw out a basin of dirty water (no plumbing). In the door stood a big dark man with a moustache, in Levis, and next to him a small, dark, short-haired person also in Levis, whom we took to be a boy our age. It was Hemingway come to call. We tactfully withdrew, and debated whether we ought to be responsible for entertaining the boy. The boy was his second wife, the sophisticated "rich bitch" of *A Moveable Feast* who stole him away from his first love in Paris. It was the beginning of Hemingway's infatuation with the guns and machismo of the West that ended tragically in Idaho so many years later.

A longer-staying guest at the Bar BC during the last days of my father's connection with it was the then Mrs. Sinclair Lewis. Lewis was another literary acquaintance, but he himself did not come west. Gracie (his first wife was always called that, as he was called Red) was beautiful, animated, and interested in higher things. She had been the model for her husband's heroines from *Main Street* to *Dodsworth*. Her cultural aspirations that had at first impressed her husband had ended by irritating him. He drank; they were separated. She came to the ranch with their son, Wells. We Burt children were supposed to dude-wrangle him, but I am afraid we did a rough job. We thought him a golden-haired momma's boy and were not kind. His almost daily office was to wait for the mail and deliver to his mother letters from her current suitor whose name was Casanova. Rich grist for the overactive gossip mills of the Bar B C. She later married Count Casanova who in fact could not have been more discreet and respectable.

The high point of that summer was an amateur movie made on the ranch with Gracie as photogenic heroine and Bill Howard as hero. I don't remember who actually shot it, nor do I remember the plot, if any. Tucker Bispham played an Old Man of the Mountains, with queer hat, bits of fur stuck about him, and mismatched dogs on leash. Bill Howard was a dude notable for his poor horsemanship—mounting from the wrong side, riding with his reins held way out. We were all in stitches for weeks. I remember nothing of the completed film, which I believe I saw in the East at the Amory's; but I do remember the hilarity of the filming. I wonder if there is a print of it somewhere?

An early visitor at the Three Rivers was the South African writer Stuart Cloete. He had just become famous with his *Turning Wheels* saga of the Boers and my father had asked him to the new ranch. One summer of the early thirties we received a telegram saying, "We are arriving." Since Cloete was unmarried, the "we" was a puzzler. "We" turned out to be a diminutive sprite nicknamed Tiny, with the smallest waist ever seen on a woman, who later became his wife but was not married to him then. The respectabilities were ruffled, but the two were lodged together and nobody seemed to mind. It was the beginning of a long family friendship, but not of Cloete's infatuation with the West. I don't remember that he ever came back.

Another subject of the King, though not really a literary one, who made his mark as a visitor at Three Rivers was an Anglo-Irishman named William Teeling. My parents had met him at a writers' conference in Missoula, Montana. Then driving back through Yellowstone, they saw him trudging along the road with a stick and bundle over his shoulder. He was dressed in a strange black tramp outfit with Charlie Chaplin as his model. He was hitchhiking from British Columbia to New Orleans. He planned to buy a bicycle there and pedal east. He had been sent to Canada by a Roman Catholic organization to make a study and report on the Doukhobors and other odd religious sects. The money ran out, however, and he was making his way back home on foot.

He was full of English public-school manners and style and had wonderful tales of the Doukhobors. According to him, they were refugee Russian sectarians who ran around naked and blew each other up with dynamite, all as part of their religion. Helen Bispham, as a result of Teeling, named her favorite horse Doukhobor. He, of course, ended up being called Duke. Teeling made an instant social success. He was invited back to stay with the Reeds and the Amorys and his hitchhiking days were over.

He was somewhat less popular with my sister, who made up his cabin for him each morning. He took a daily bath in his tin tub and left the dirty water for her to throw out (Water Water O God). Finally she heaved the tub up on his bed and left it there. He got the message.

I saw him later on at a weekend in Tuxedo at the Amory's where his habit of dropping dirty clothes on the floor to be picked up and washed was part of the domestic routine. Tying his tie in the evening before dinner, he would practice witty epigrams in the mirror and then, by gum, actually manage to work them into the conversation. He gave a great final cocktail party in New York to which he invited everyone he had met in America—Palm Beach call girls in leopard skin coats, Dr. Katharine Merritt, the Burts. He wrote a book called, appropriately enough, *American Stew,* and then went home to become a member of Parliament in the Roman Catholic interest as Sir William. I never saw him in this later phase.

More strictly literary were the Alfred Knopfs and the Bernard De Votos. I remember the Knopfs arriving for lunch in great high-peaked white Western hats over their dark, fierce faces and filling the dining room with New York animation. A small De Voto boy insisted on running into the corral among the horses, much to my father's fury. Finally my father broke down and shouted, "All right, you little son-of-a-bitch, go in there and get killed!," after which the boy's conduct was model and he adored my father as a Real Westerner.

There were many other such drop-ins (at the Bar BC, guests were characterized as "drop-ins," short visits; or "lay-overs," longer-term dudes). A lay-over was Wallace Stegner who spent a summer at Three Rivers in Katharine Merritt's cabin, during the Mangum period. The Stegners had with them their son Page, then a thin boy of about eleven. Among the numberless Mangum progeny was a boy of the same age called Conrad, a red-haired character of great self-assurance and charm. He and Page played about together, and when the Stegners left, they took Conrad with them as a companion for Page. He always called my father by his first name. I remember him as he left with his skinny arm around my father's shoulder saying, "Well, goodbye, Struthers. Take care of yourself." The arrangement evidently did not work out and Conrad went back to Virgin or Hurricane or wherever his particular Mangums were located. Page grew up to become a writer too.

A more exotic literary guest was the philosopher-essayist Irwin Edman. Bald and almost blind, he looked like some rather amiable wild creature of the mole variety. He was always falling into ditches and losing his way in the sagebrush on the way to dinner. At dinner he elevated the conversation with his humor and erudition. Since various daughters of Maxwell Perkins were visiting the Three Rivers at this time, it was a summer of fairly heavy literary associations. I remember a picnic up on the ridge, where we sat around on an old poncho with an old volume of Tennyson's poems in hand, discussing poetic subjects. The view was glorious as ever, but I never was sure Irwin could see the scenery well enough to appreciate it. The picnic was partly memorialized in one of the short essays in his *Philosopher's Holiday*.

An enormous amount has been written about Jackson Hole, but much of it is lost in the files of newspapers and magazines. Both Burts and Hough wrote many short pieces with a Western background. One of the best of the periodical writers was Joe Jones, that Founding Father of the park, whose vivid recountings of his experiences as gambler and as homesteader in the *Saturday Evening Post* have already been mentioned. Equally indigenous and evocative, but also not yet in book form, are the pieces, two of them published in the *Atlantic Monthly*, written by native Frances Judge about her pioneer great-grandmother, grandmother, and mother. "Classic" is certainly the proper word for these glowing biographies of remarkable ranch women — tough, able, emotional, stoic, and above all imaginative and humorous. Let anyone who thinks of pioneers as "dour" or "drab" just read these portraits of real people. Unfortunately, neither of these local writers has been properly republished—a defect that must certainly be remedied soon.

More fortunate have been the writings of at least three other local women writers: Sally Carrighar, Margaret Murie, and Josephine Fabian. Sally Carrighar's *One Day at Teton Marsh*, published by Knopf back in 1947, could also be called classic, and has taken its place in the permanent library of readable and knowledgeable American nature writing. Though never a true settler in the valley, Sally Carrighar kept up her connections there for many years and her book is certainly a local product. Margaret Murie, however, is very much a resident. Her *Wapiti Wilderness* (1966) continues her autobiography as first described in *Two in the Far North* (1965). *Wapiti Wilderness* tells what happened when that famous family of naturalists, the quartet of half-brothers Olaus and Adolf Murie and their half-sister wives, came to Jackson Hole and established themselves there as first citizens of natural science and conservation.

Another famous family of naturalists long resident in the Hole is that of the Craighead twins, Frank and John, who have written profusely—with a special emphasis on native birds. The scientist Fritiof Fryxell has written beautifully as well as knowledgeably about the Tetons. There are and have been many other such nature writers, though most of their work is in periodicals or pamphlets.

Two women, Elizabeth Wied Hayden and Josephine Fabian, have made significant contributions to local human, as opposed to natural, history. Betty has written articles on aspects of early settlement. Josephine has made an invaluable collection of tape recordings by old-timers, including that one of Elena Hunt. She has also written a book of historical fiction called *The Jackson's Hole Story* (1963) built around the flamboyant caravan that brought President Chester A. Arthur through the valley in 1883.

Three good histories of Jackson Hole have been published recently. One by Frank Calkins (Knopf, 1973) relies heavily on the invaluable resources of Slim Lawrence, who knows more about the history of the region than anyone living. Another by David I. Saylor, *Jackson Hole, Wyoming: In the Shadow of the Tetons* (Oklahoma, 1970), is written more from a Park Service point of view. A third, *Along the Ramparts of the Tetons* (Colorado, 1978), by Robert B. Betts, stresses the earlier history of the Hole. Like painters of the Tetons or photographers, writers about these mountains flourish; but so far none seems to have rivaled the reputations of past masters.

Even music, least indigenous of all the fine arts to the West, except in the form of folk songs, is now triumphant in the Hole. Major credit must be given to the Baroness of Melody Ranch, Consuela von Gontard; but many local music lovers were also active in promoting a summer orchestra in 1962. Concerts were held in the high-school auditorium or at the Jackson Lake Lodge, and even out in the middle of the square in Jackson. Ernest Hagen, who had conducted an orchestra in Casper, Wyoming, was the first conductor in Jackson Hole, and from the very beginning standards were high; but there were the usual struggles, financial and personal. It was not until the orchestra was taken over by its present conductor, Ling Tung, in 1967, and moved up to the ski resort of Teton Village in 1969 that it became firmly established.

A few vignettes stand out in my memory: the performance of a work by George Hufsmith, the composer conducting at the Jackson Lake Lodge, was one of them. This was, as far as I know, the first work by a resident composer to be played in the Hole. Hufsmith has been a prominent insurance man in Jackson and a state representative; but he is also a trained musician, having studied at Yale and under the Brazilian composer Villa Lobos.

Another memory dates from the time when Hagen was conductor. He mysteriously came to call one night at the Burt cabin on the Three Rivers. What prompted him I do not know. I suspect he wanted some sort of financial or political or even personal help but was too shy to come out with it. In any case, I'm afraid he didn't get it, whatever it was.

Later on, in the time of Tung, I remember a late summer concert at the high school in Jackson. It was a fearful rainy night. Football practice had begun. In the middle of the slow movement of a Beethoven symphony the football team clattered into the auditorium in their cleats, fresh from muddy practice, headed for their dressing rooms in the same building. When they were safely in, the manager stood with his back against the dressing room door to be sure that they wouldn't emerge while music was going on.

At one concert in the big blue tent that was the orchestra's first home at Teton Village, all the electricity went out, so the performance took place in the romantic firefly glow of dozens of lanterns—electric, kerosene, and candle. Now a magnificent new hall has been built and partly paid for and the summer festival is one of the best in the country. Half a dozen orchestral concerts are surrounded by a galaxy of chamber music evenings; musicians come to play from all over the United States; and in fifteen years the Hole has developed from scratch into a Tanglewood of the West.

Ling Tung, the conductor, was born in Shanghai, China, of a family all of whom seem to have become professional musicians. He still has a winter base in Philadelphia, but also has conducted the Hong Kong Symphony Orchestra. He has toured the world as guest conductor and has been particularly popular in Japan, the first Chinese to conduct there. Since he does not speak much Japanese and not all Japanese speak English, much less Chinese, he has sometimes faced communication barriers. A peculiarly Oriental way of surmounting these barriers was discovered: he was able to draw the ideograph symbolizing his idea in the air. Although the spoken version of the ideograph may be quite different in Japanese and Chinese, the thought as written is the same.

Jackson is now loaded with art galleries, music stores (one called "Papa Bach"), and craft shops. Reginald and Gladys Laubin, permanent summer residents, perform their authentically inspired versions of American Indian dances. Articles continue to pour from the press, photographs and paintings from the studio; many of these appear beautifully reproduced in the summer issue of *Teton Magazine*. Sooner or later all this artistic humus is bound to produce some sort of native product of high caliber. Living writers like Frances Judge and photographers like Ansel Adams set a high standard. As for musical composition, Hufsmith is still writing. As far as I know, however, I am the only native-*born* composer whose works have been performed at the festival—a sonatina for bassoon and an "Elegy of Lycidas" for orchestra, in 1974 and 1975 respectively. Some day Jackson Hole may be as famous for its artists in some form or other as it is now for its mountains.

Meanwhile, a most exotic and non-native intruder in the valley from early days has been Hollywood. A whole book could and should be devoted to this constant series of often ludicrous invasions. My mother was, I suspect, the very first person to make connections between the Hole and Hollywood. As writer of *The Branding Iron,* she was summoned to Hollywood in 1920 by Samuel Goldwyn along with half-a-dozen other best-selling writers. Goldwyn had a grandiose plan for elevating the taste of the still-infant industry by injecting literary tone into it. The writers summoned were a mixed bag. Gertrude Atherton, grande dame of San Francisco writing, was the highest toned. There is a wonderful group photograph, Atherton sitting disdainfully in the front row, her face turned away from the camera, her parasol out at an angle, next to my mother. Mary Roberts Rinehart sits beyond; Sam Goldwyn stands behind. The only one of the group who stayed to elevate the industry was Rupert Hughes, uncle of Howard. It was because of Uncle Rupert that Howard left Texas and oil drills and became involved in motion pictures, aviation, sex, and billions.

A good many of my mother's novels and stories were made into lurid silent films, and the old cardroom of the Bar BC, where I once slept, was later on covered with stills of these movies—actors in heavy makeup glaring through artificial snowstorms. So when star Mary Miles Minter descended on the Hole in 1922 to make *The Cowboy and the Lady,* my mother was already an old Hollywood hand. Mary graciously received the yokels as she reclined on leopard skins in an Arabian tent up near the base of the Tetons. My mother attended one of these levees. Mary couldn't seem to recall whether she had played in one of my mother's films or not. "Ah, I never can remember the authors of my pictures." "And I can never remember the actresses in mine," my mother gleefully retorted.

Mary returned to Hollywood and disgrace. She was involved in a dreadful scandal of sex and murder that put an end to her career. The Burt family's connection with films dwindled and died less spectacularly, although a later talking version of *The Branding Iron* called, I believe, something like *I Want My Man* and transposed to Switzerland, was something of a success. The branding episode of *The Branding Iron* was at least preserved intact (jealous husband brands wife to keep her on his range).

Tom Mix made an "oater" in the Hole in 1925. In 1930 *The Big Trail* tore up the valley, a major production that flopped, ruining everyone concerned except the beautiful, if not very animated, young male lead whose first starring vehicle it was: John Wayne. Dick Winger acted as quartermaster general for this epic, which involved thousands of head of stock, hundreds of extras, and many permanent locations. One of these was a perfect replica of an Indian village with real Indians. Flanking the front door of the main cabin at the Three Rivers were two plaster reproductions of Indian corn grinders. The movie was a godsend to an already Depression-ridden Hole, if not exactly welcomed by ranchers trying to hire hay hands. I remember going to a location on Spread Creek. Indians were supposed to come charging down a bluff. The Indians — rugged cowboy extras sprayed with brown paint, riding bareback — charged down, whooping and hollering, were tripped by guy wires, painfully picked themselves up, and then had to do it all over again. And again and again. There was always something wrong. At one point, I believe, even then, an airplane appeared in the sky over the Indians. It was fascinating for a while but got boring. Dick Winger's scathing tales of mix-up and mayhem on location lasted him a lifetime.

Later Westerns made in the Hole were more successful, if never as extravagant. The best was *Shane*, still something of a classic, made in 1951 and starring Alan Ladd. That same summer two other good Westerns, *Jubal* with Glenn Ford and *The*

Big Sky with Kirk Douglas, were also being shot. The Hole was stuffed with stars that season: Glenn Ford, Ernest Borgnine, and Rod Steiger at the Triangle X; Kirk Douglas all over the Snake River on rafts; Alan Ladd, Jean Arthur, and Van Heflin in and out of the Wort Hotel. We saw *Shane* in Chicago, and as Alan Ladd rode off at the end towards the Tetons my father said, "He's going to look for a cook."

Wallace Beery, after his startling first visit by plane to the Elbo, became a yearly summer visitor and had his own place on Jackson Lake. He too made movies in the Hole, but his most notable performance was in 1943 at the time when FDR created the National Monument. He mounted his horse (the canard is that he needed a stepladder) and, attended by photographers and reporters, rode across the flats brandishing a six-shooter and defying the government's right to interfere with the range. Most mistaken and perhaps last of the big Hollywood invasions was that filming of *Spencer's Mountain* in 1963. Henry Fonda was wasted on this one, and Jackson Holers were generally disgusted by the lack of authenticity produced by the attempt to graft an Appalachian tale on Wyoming scenery. They were annoyed, but they were also employed. A short-lived television serial, *The Monroes*, was also shot in 1970 along the banks of the Snake. We used to watch it for the scenery; it was nice in a corny, folksy way.

Since *Spencer's Mountain*, only Charlton Heston's recent *Mountain Man* seems to carry on the tradition of grand-scale, old-fashioned Hollywood in the Hole. Those days too seem to have become a part of that permanently vanishing Old West. Hollywood in Jackson Hole may not have been "native," but it was certainly picturesque and good for many and many a laugh on the part of those same "natives."

A more intimate and less gaudy embrace between the Hole

and culture than that provided by Hollywood has been the trickle of Burt poetry written in and about Wyoming. Although never a famous poet, my father did have a reputation during the 1920s evidenced by magazine publications, reprints, inclusion in anthologies, and the success of his later books. His very first appearance between covers was in 1914 when Houghton Mifflin produced a mousy gray volume of poetry called *In the High Hills*. He felt the poetry to be in the nature of juvenilia, although he was thirty in 1911. Despite the title poem there are comparatively few Western references in the book. The character of his poetry was always that of the English Georgians (the period from Robert Louis Stevenson to Rupert Brooke) even when applied to the Rocky Mountains.

His second and third books of poetry, *Songs and Portraits* (1920) and *When I Grew Up to Middle Age* (1925), were a different matter. Most of these poems had appeared first in magazines; several were reprinted or anthologized afterward; and many of them were specifically Western. They still exhibited the piquant (or incongruous) blend of Georgianism and outdoorsmanship on the order of Henry van Dyke, but in a more mature fashion.

Songs and Portraits is full of poems with family references. It is dedicated to my Aunt Jean, a suicide of 1918, with a dedicatory poem, and there are other poems to my mother, my sister (aged four), and me (aged six). In the third book, however, the best known of his Western poems appeared, notably "Five Songs of Wyoming" ("When I have been too long away from Pilgrim Creek and John O'Day,/When I have been a year or so from where the tumbling waters go,/From Cottonwood and Crystal Creek and Soda Fork and Buffalo . . .") and the best known of them all, the "Pack-Trip: Suite." It was at this time, around the middle of the 1920s, that his poetic reputation was at its highest. I remember once sending a telegram home as an adolescent. When I wrote my father's name and address, the high-toned girl back of the telegraph desk asked, "The poet?"

In the thirties he wrote and published almost no poetry. Then the approaches and outbreak of World War II stirred him to produce his last book, *War Songs*, very specifically patriotic. These poems were published, with a good deal of fanfare, in important magazines, were set to music, and in general were an active part of the "war effort." Some of the poems of this final book also had Western overtones, notably "September" and "John Erth."

The tradition has continued with my own poetry. A spate of magazine publications during the war and two volumes afterward, *Rooms in a House* (1947) and *Question on a Kite* (1950), contained various poems inspired by and written in the West. Since then the flow has gone on—a span from at least 1912 to 1982, not so much claiming quantity or quality as continuity, a current indigenous footnote to the already sufficiently curious cultural history of Jackson Hole.

It has been well over fifty years since *The Diary of a Dude Wrangler* was published in 1924. Fifty years before that, as of the early 1870s, a New West of the cowboy and the frontier and the false-front cowtown superseded the Old West of the trapper and emigrant train and the military fort. As of 1824 there was in turn a New West, the climax of beaver trapping and the trapper's rendezvous. In 1774 the West still belonged to the Indians, Indians most of whom were New West fifty years before that when (perhaps) as of the 1720s they were emigrating from their Middle Western river valleys and taking over the culture of the Plains Indians. The year 1974 was the climax of the Tourist West.

What next? For it would seen that every fifty years represents a different chapter in the region's history, the climax of one phase, the beginnings of another. I have lived through one chapter of it—the transition from what was still cattle and frontier to what is now tourist boom. It's to this latter age that I really belong, despite my attachments to the older period. I have not been a frontiersman but essentially a tourist, a summer visitor. My sixty years have been spent on dude ranches or summer places like the Bar BC or the Three Rivers. Most of the people I have known have been either other summer visitors or those who worked in summer businesses. So, whether I like it or not, I belong to this special West of 1920-1980, the Tourist West.

The fact that I don't like it is part of the tragedy of the tourist. "Each man kills the thing he loves," and nobody more unwillingly but more surely than the tourist. The minute the tourist steps on the scene he destroys it. When the tourist enters the wilderness, it's no longer the wilderness he's there to appreciate, simply because he's there. When the tourist comes to see the Old West, he creates a New West just by his presence. What the tourist wants to see is what he himself is *not*. But he inevitably brings himself with him. The tourist seeking the exotic setting intrudes and makes the setting just that much less exotic. The descent from the genuine to the fake-tourist-trap begins. The extraordinary he came to see becomes the ordinary he is. Jackson, which was a genuine enough dusty, bare, ramshackle cowtown in 1920 (and of course, brand new then, hardly more than a dozen years old), is now a prosperous, gussied-up, luxurious enough tourist mecca. It is really a lot prettier, but certainly not what could be called "genuine."

It is at least to the credit of Jackson Hole and the West as a whole that, tourist-ridden though it may be, it still isn't "ordinary." The colors may have changed, but they are still colorful. The crazy juxtaposition of high-toned and low-toned, of culture and crudeness, of old-time and new-fangled still exists in the 1980s as it did in the 1920s. The remoteness, the frontier quality is gone forever; but the regional quality, the Western quality is just as strong as ever. Nobody for a moment could confuse Jackson Hole with, say, central New Jersey. Tawdry it may be, just as some of it always was, but not drab.

At the same time, as the once New West of 1870 gradually evolved into the Old West of Wister, the United States as a whole was converted from an agricultural to an industrial nation. It was the impact of that industrial world, largely in the form of visitors from it, that transformed the still agricultural Hole between 1920 and 1970. The Three Rivers was linked to industrial America by means of the REA power lines, by the great new roads that now lead from Togwotee Pass down to Jackson, up to Yellowstone, and beyond. The airport makes what was once a long six-day train journey from the East a matter of less than a full day. Jackson Lake Lodge provides anonymous comfort for thousands of well-heeled voyagers who can look out at the scenery without ever being part of it in any way. As in every place, Mass moves in to oust Class, always with a lowering of standards, a coarsening of tastes, a blurring of outlines, a crudeness of effects. But the elegant summer-long dude of 1920 was still a tourist and represented the same sort of corruption. The dudes were just the advance guard of the barbarian invasion.

As for the "natives," they have ceased to be "roughnecks," though certainly not yet "tenderfeet." Compared to the horrifying starvation and back-breaking drudgery of the unsuccessful homesteader of 1907 as described by Joe Jones in

his *Saturday Evening Post* article, the present native takes for
granted cars and winter heat and summer pleasures like boating on the lake or meals in really good restaurants. The all-
year-round employment created by the opening up of winter
skiing evens the once drastic imbalance between summer and
winter prosperity in the valley. It also destroys the picturesque
isolation described by Donald Hough or used by my mother
as a background for *Snow Blind* and *Hidden Creek*. The sump-
tuous modern villas around Teton Village or between Jackson
and Wilson on their expensive lots with their terraces and plate
glass vistas may not be native or Old West but they are certainly magnificent. The people who live in them love Jackson
Hole too, are there because they love it, and, if it isn't the
Jackson Hole that people of my dispensation love, it certainly
has its own glamours and glories.

Would things have been different if Rockefeller and the
park hadn't saved the valley? Obviously. One can see what
would have happened by looking at what has happened around
Jackson. Would things have been different if the vague dream
of the local conservationists for some sort of "museum on the
hoof" could have been realized? I rather suspect not. It was
too unrealizable a dream, too difficult to achieve and administer. What would the Hole be like if it weren't for the fame
of the Tetons? Being at the south entrance of Yellowstone,
it would have been overrun, but without the kind of protection that the park gives it. There would surely never have
been a chance, given its location, that the Hole wouldn't have
been crowded, could still be remote or isolated. Could it still
be some sort of Dream Hole if it had been somewhere else
and without the fatal attraction of its peaks?

Perhaps a real Western Shangri-La could exist in some less-
traveled part of the country. But then maybe the threats of

outer exploitation and inner corruption would be at the stage they were in Wyoming in 1920 before conservation became a formidable force, before anyone knew what the tourist boom was going to be like. Jackson Hole is no Perfect Basin. A lot of the development has been and continues to be cheap, ill planned, disgusting. An influx of millions every summer continues to present its desperate problems of human erosion. Nonetheless, the Hole also still manages to maintain its individual character, its spectacular looks, its own feisty cross-grained Westernism. Because local businessmen play golf doesn't mean that lots of the "natives" aren't still pretty native.

What in the world will it all be like in 2024, a century after *Diary of a Dude Wrangler?* I can hope that whoever writes it up as of then, looking back with nostalgia on my Old West of 1920-80, will be able to notice, given inevitable enormous changes, approximately the same things—the persistence of scenery, character, and Western regionalism, if not of the frontier. Shortages of fuel, for instance, may collapse the automobile tourist boom as the change to silk hats collapsed the beaver boom. The Hole might once more become remote, full of ghost motels. But I can hope the mountains and the sky and the "doom" of the river and the game in the hills may survive the traumas of the next half century, and that Jackson Hole may still remain breathtakingly beautiful.

INDEX

Jackson Hole Journal,
designed by Bill Cason, was composed in Goudy Old Style by the
University of Oklahoma Press and printed offset on 55-pound Glat-
felter B-31, a permanized sheet, with presswork by Cushing-Malloy,
Inc., and binding by John H. Dekker & Sons.